of **LOVE**
and **PARIS**

*Historic, Romantic and
Obsessive Liaisons*

JOHN BAXTER

MUSEYON

New York

Library of Congress Cataloging-in-Publication Data

Names: Baxter, John, 1939- author.
Title: Of Love and Paris : historic, romantic and obsessive liaisons / John Baxter.
Description: New York : Museyon, [2023] | Includes index.
Identifiers: LCCN 2023018709 (print) | LCCN 2023018710 (ebook) | ISBN
9781940842721 (paperback) | ISBN 9781940842738 (ebook)
Subjects: LCSH: Paris (France)--Social life and customs. |
Love--France--Paris--History. | Sex--France--Paris--History. | BISAC:
TRAVEL / Europe / France
Classification: LCC DC715 .B3168 2023 (print) | LCC DC715 (ebook) | DDC
944/.36--dc23/eng/20230609
LC record available at https://lccn.loc.gov/2023018709
LC ebook record available at https://lccn.loc.gov/2023018710

Published in the United States and Canada by:
Museyon Inc.
333 East 45th Street
New York, NY 10017

Museyon is a registered trademark.
Visit us online at www.museyon.com

Cover: Streetcorner, Paris 1934. Photo © Fred Stein / Bridgeman Images

ISBN 978-1-940842-72-1 (Print)
ISBN 978-1-940842-73-8 (eBook)

Printed in China

For Marie Dominique and Louise

CONTENTS

INTRODUCTION

On Paris and Love . . .

". . . and it ought to make us feel ashamed when we talk like we know what we're talking about when we talk about love."

Raymond Carver, *What We Talk About When We Talk About Love*

The Perfumed Battlefield

"She wanted to die," wrote Gustave Flaubert of his self-deluded heroine Emma Bovary, "but she also wanted to live in Paris." The city invites such extremes of emotion and attracts the people who experience them. As New York and London acted as magnets for anyone anxious to succeed in business, Paris drew those who desired to express their feelings, either in art or in the way they lived. Among the most powerful of those impulses is love—intellectual, spiritual, carnal. And Paris, when it comes to that complex and elusive emotion, is internationally recognised as the world capital.

Reasons are not hard to find. Conquered by the Romans, colonized by Christianity, invaded by the English, inherited by the Bourbon kings, from whom it liberated itself in the revolution of 1789, only to be swept up in the imperial ambitions of the Napoléons, then forced to endure two wars on its soil, as well as four years of German occupation before being absorbed into the European Union, France has been a plaything of history. The experience created a culture of acceptance and acquiescence.

Some historians, not entirely as a compliment, called France "the woman of Europe," and the label stuck. It may explain why, though Britain has John Bull and the United States Uncle Sam, France is symbolized by a female, albeit militant, beginning with Joan of Arc, followed by revolutionary heroine Marianne, a bust of whom, based on Delacroix's image of Liberty from his 1830 canvas (and modeled by the decade's most popular TV or movie star), is displayed in every town hall. The French pay lip service to the aggressive aspect of this archetype, but as a peaceful, rural nation, not temperamentally given to settling problems by force—an American general sneered that, "Going to war without France is like going hunting without an accordion"—they prefer to prevail by the more feminine traits of intelligence, charm and cunning. Proficient diplomats, they made French the language of negotiation and compromise. Matters of state were settled behind the scenes, and, as often as not, in the bedroom, which became, for the French, "a perfumed battlefield."

A Rose is a Rose is a....?

Traditionally, the adjective "French" implies intricacy and complexity, not only in clothing and food, but also in manners and, naturally, sex. Hence "Frenching" and "French kissing," the "French letter"—a condom disguised in a paper packet—and its refinement, the "French tickler," not forgetting, of course, the "French disease" of syphilis. One would have expected the language of love to also be French; *foufoune* for vagina, *bite* [pronounced "beet"] for an erect penis, *pipe* ["peep"] for fellatio and the now-antique *gamahuche* for all forms of oral sex. But in his 1782 *Les Liaisons Dangereuses,* a classic tale of sexual duplicity and intrigue, Pierre Cholderlos de Laclos suggests a reason why these and similar words don't appear in the lexicon of erotica. "As with every other science," explains the cynical Valmont as he seduces an eager Cécile de Volange, "the first principle is to make sure you

Les Liaisons Dangereuses by
Georges Barbier, 1920s

call everything by its proper name. Now I think we might begin
with one or two Latin terms . . . "

As Latin was the language of science and medicine, sexual ter-
minology logically derived from Rome, including those "Latin
terms"—fellatio, cunnilingus, vagina, penis, sperm, coitus and
their numerous derivatives—but Italy's attempts at any more sub-
tle distinctions ended there. It was left to the French to elucidate
love's many forms, only a few of them defined by anatomy.

French medieval writers were the first to distinguish between
amor honestus (honest *i.e.*, physical love) and *fin amor* (refined or abstract love). The love of an abstraction, for example one's home-

land, was not the same as love for a wife or husband, while neither resembled what Shakespeare in *Hamlet* called, in a pun on the most common slang term in English for a vagina, "country matters." The traditional marriage service, first set out in the 1662 *Book of Common Prayer,* clarified the widening gap between the two by attempting to disguise the sexual nature of marriage as a metaphoric abstraction, "instituted of God in the time of man's innocency, signifying unto us the mystical union that is betwixt Christ and his Church . . . and therefore not by any to be enterprised, nor taken in hand unadvisedly, lightly, or wantonly, to satisfy men's carnal lusts and appetites, like brute beasts that have no understanding."

By employing metaphor and simile, the language of *fin amor,* renamed in the 19th century "courtly love," allowed one to talk about love while actually appearing to speak of something else. Troubadours travelling the courts of Europe sang of their love for the Virgin when it was another and more available woman they had in mind. The language of flowers was equally effective. The 12th century narrative poem *Roman de la Rose* depicted Love as a walled garden surrounded by dangers which the lover must defeat before he can enter. Seventeenth century poet Charles Beys's *La Jouissance Imparfaite* used flowers to find poetry in a woman trying to hide her nudity:

Then with her lovely hands she does conceal

Those wonders chance so kindly did reveal.

In vain, alas, her nimble fingers strove

To keep her beauties from my greedy love

Guarding her breasts, they do her lips expose,

To save a lily she must lose a rose.

Sometimes the floral comparison assumed a sinister tone, with apparently flattering imagery disguising duplicity, violence, even disease. Eighteenth century British visionary William Blake wrote:

O rose, thou are sick.

The invisible worm

That flies in the night

In the howling storm

Has found out thy bed

Of crimson joy

And his dark secret love

Does thy life destroy.

Intense feelings became less threatening if seen as aspects of the natural world. Seventeenth century French courtier Catherine de Rambouillet created an *aide memoire* called the *Carte de Tendre*. The map of an imaginary country called *Tendre* or Sweetness, its amorous geography included districts called New Friendship and Mutual Admiration, the villages of Pretty Verse and Love Letter, but also Indifference Mountain.

Not everyone was in sympathy with this use of nature. Nineteenth century British art historian John Ruskin coined the term "pathetic fallacy" to denigrate the manner in which such poets as Wordsworth used weather in particular to mirror emotions. Critics claim that Ruskin's distaste simply reflected his horror of sensuality. (He shunned sex and found the female body, and in particular pubic hair, disgusting. His wife divorced him on the grounds that their marriage was never consummated.) In fact, the use of parallels between nature and the emotions has a long and durable history. Shakespeare's *Richard III* opens with Richard praising a new dynasty for turning a "winter of discontent" into "glorious summer." Expanding this train of thought, the French spoke of love at first sight as *un coup de foudre*—a clap of thunder. Silent cinema represented emotion with pounding surf and surrender with an opening flower, while Brigitte Bardot, in a notorious duet with then-lover Serge Gainsbourg, murmured, "You are the wave. I am the naked island," and he responded, "Like the undecided wave, I go—I go and I come."

Once Upon a Time

Twentieth century sociologists Bruno Bettelheim and Joseph Campbell showed that fables, an extension of metaphor, also often revealed more than did statistics about the nature of a society. A story from before the time of written language can have remarkable longevity, each generation adapting it to its own use.

Jean Cocteau's *Beauty and the Beast,* 1946

Among the most durable of such stories is *Beauty and the Beast.* That it employs the language of flowers and the symbolism of the *Roman de la Rose* suggests the period in which it was composed. The first modern retelling, that of Gabrielle-Suzanne de Villeneuve, dates from 1740 but the most famous, by Jeanne-Marie Prince de Beaumont, was written a century later. In their essentials, all versions are the same. Beauty, a young woman, sacrifices herself to save her father, condemned to death for picking a rose from the walled garden of a monster. Against all odds, the Beast spares Beauty and allows her to live in his castle. She realizes that his features disguise a man who has been placed under a spell that may only be lifted by a woman who loves him as he is.

Prince de Beaumont shaped her version to serve a social purpose. At a time of arranged marriages, when young women were often urged to take older, richer partners rather than the impecunious boys they might have preferred, *La Belle et la Bête* suggested that, with a little imagination, the new wife might discover a prince behind the paunch. And even if they did not, they could console themselves with the chateau, the servants, and a husband ready to satisfy (almost) all their needs.

Jean Cocteau's 1946 film updated the fable for a postwar generation. The Beast is played by Cocteau's lover and protégé Jean Marais while Josette Day as Belle already prefers her father to the rowdies who court her. The Beast's estate becomes a new version of the medieval realm of Love, while Beauty is the virgin with a father complex succumbing to the lure of forbidden sex. The moment when she enters the chateau, gliding, her feet seeming not to touch the floor, along a corridor lit by *flambeaux* held by living arms jutting from the walls, would forever be associated with stories of troubled love. Jacques Demy used the image in his film *The Umbrellas of Cherbourg* to signify the ill-starred devotion of Catherine Deneuve to her garage mechanic boyfriend, and it was resurrected for TV appearances by Jane Birkin when she celebrated Serge Gainsbourg's songs, reminding audiences that the couple's life together replicated the myth.

With a Kiss

A popular joke says that, in a nightmare world, policemen would be German, car mechanics French and cooks and lovers English, while in Utopia the policemen would be English, the car mechanics German and the cooks and lovers French. Evidence is scant, however, that the French are as naturally endowed in the bedroom as Germans in the garage or the British at New Scotland Yard. Where they do excel is in technique. As Alan Jay Lerner and Frederick Loewe put it in *My Fair Lady*, "The French never care what they do, actually, as long as they *pronounce* it properly." This imprecision has given the French an ambiguous reputation among countries with less evolved sexual practices. Not only do the French decline to use those robust "Latin terms;" their sexual methods are also unconventional, in particular employing lips and tongue in an inappropriate manner. One gibe even combined this accusation with an attack on the French distaste for military confrontation. "The French they are a funny race/They fight with their feet and they fuck with their face."

No act between individuals is more significant in French society than the kiss. Depending on how and where it is bestowed, by whom, in what number and with what degree of passion, it can signify one's social level, familial connection and community standing, as well as those subtler shades of meaning that all French children learn in infancy and which become, by adolescence, second nature.

The kiss defines the relationship of those who administer it and creates a basis for communication. As in nature, females make the running. On first meeting a woman, it's usual to shake hands, but on parting, if the meeting has not been drop-dead disastrous, she will offer her cheek. Between females, two kisses are standard, a third indicates genuine pleasure, while enduring affection demands a fourth, and even, exceptionally, a touch on the lips. Among men, the kiss is reserved for close friends or relatives—"kissing cousins"—but also, paradoxically, for formal ceremonies: weddings, funerals, the conferring of honors. In such cases, "sealed with a kiss," means what it says. As official as a rubber stamp, the kiss confirms legality. Nobody watching Charles de Gaulle hinging his mantis-like frame to plant two smackers on the cheeks of a *poilu* just presented with a Croix de Guerre could possibly imagine he meant anything more by it than comradely respect.

Eating

"Eating" to signify oral sex is among the ugliest of American coinings. "French kissing" first appeared in English around 1923 to describe a kiss that employed both lips and tongue; something at which the French, traditionally, were adept. Before long, however, it came to mean oral sex. When, in 1933, actress Mary Astor confided to her diary that taking an open carriage ride through Central Park with playwright George S. Kaufman permitted them to "pet and French right out in the open," everyone got the picture. Incidentally, it's not only in English that meanings change. Time has also transformed the meaning of *baiser*. Once "kiss," it now means, frankly, "fuck." Today's polite form is *embrasse*.

While there's no evidence that the French invented oral sex, they soon recognized its affinity with the national culture and adopted it with enthusiasm. Not only is it, among sexual practices, the least phallocentric: in the way it deprecates vigor and exceptional physical attributes but valorizes precision, concentration and attention to detail in the attenuation of pleasure, it takes its place with the other elements of erotic expertise for which France became famous: what to say to a sexual partner and how to say it, how to dress (and undress), when, how and where to use perfume, the selection and wearing of lingerie—defined by one authority as "the artillery of the night" (and therefore, like artillery in its military use, to be employed in softening up a target as preparation for an assault) : these skills, taught to all courtesans, trickled down into the bedrooms of France, where they were perfected and refined.

The Business of Sex

France accelerated the widespread use and acceptance of sexual technique by demolishing the barriers between professional and amateur. Sodomy was legalized under the Revolution in 1790. Napoléon decriminalized prostitution in 1804, subject to certain restrictions, which, significantly, were not religious or moral but legal and medical. A prostitute had to register with the police and pass a twice-weekly medical examination. A woman found to be infected could be imprisoned until cured. To eradicate pimping and the exploitation that went with it, men could own a brothel

Women displaying their charms at a brothel

but a woman—the traditional *madame*—must be in charge of day-to-day business. Clients paid her, and she in turn paid the wages, and provided food and lodging if women "lived in."

The law also required that the appearance of *maisons de tolerance* or *maisons closes* be discreet. Shutters over the windows had to be of solid wood, and nothing should indicate what took place behind them. France never adopted the red lamp used in other countries to designate a brothel. Most were identified simply by their address; "*Le 122*," for example, referred to 122 rue du Provence. Others adopted the most bland of titles: At My Brother-in-Law's or My Uncle's Place. Annual *Guides Roses* gave their addresses, as well as cafés where girls could be found, and their specialties known.

Brothels proliferated following the change in the law. By 1810, Paris alone had 180, and within 50 years there were more than a thousand across the nation. With legality came social acceptance. Guy de Maupassant's *The House of Madame Tellier*, published in 1885, is set in a small town, where Madame Tellier's brothel is a social center.

They went there every evening about eleven o'clock, just as they would go to the club. Six or eight of them; always the same set, not fast men, but respectable tradesmen, and young men in government or some other employ, and they would drink their Chartreuse, and laugh with the girls, or else talk seriously with Madame Tellier, whom everybody respected, and then they would go home at twelve o'clock! The younger men would sometimes stay later. Madame Tellier, who came of a respectable family of peasant proprietors in the Department of the Eure, had taken up her profession, just as she would have become a milliner or dressmaker. The prejudice, which is so violent and deeply rooted in large towns, does not exist in the country places in Normandy. The peasant says 'It is a paying-business,' and he sends his daughter to keep an establishment of this character just as he would send her to keep a girls' school.

In the Paris of the *belle époque*, the itinerary of every visiting head of state included "an evening with the President of the Sénat." The time was not wasted on speeches and toasts. Instead, visitors were delivered to 12 rue Chabanais, a discreet building in the second *arrondissement,* convenient both to the Chambre des Députés and the Bibliotheque Nationale. The only hint that it housed the city's most gifted purveyors of pleasure was a sign on the restaurant opposite. "What we serve," it said, "is as good as what you get across the road."

A syndicate of businessmen and aristocrats operated La Chabanais for clients as rich and discriminating as themselves, rather as the Playboy key clubs of the 1970s provided places where businessmen could meet informally and enjoy female company. Women were chosen for charm and intelligence as well as beauty. The owners also enjoyed decorating their home-away-from-home, purchasing entire rooms from exhibitions of foreign design and transferring the contents to La Chabanais, earning it the title "The House of All Nations." American expatriate Harry Crosby gave his approval to "the Persian and the Russian and the Turkish and the Japanese and the Spanish rooms, and the bathroom with mirrored walls and mirrored ceilings, and the 30 harlots waiting in the salon."

No effort was spared for the comfort of its clients. They even filtered its water supply so that no speck of grit might impair their pleasure. Among those enjoying these refinements was the future King Edward VII of Great Britain, for whom, because of his obesity, the management designed a "love chair" that permitted easy access for oral and other forms of sex. It also created an ornate copper bath in which his favorite prostitute could splash in champagne while the prince and his cronies sat around, occasionally dipping out a glass.

The best brothels had good wine cellars and, in some cases, restaurants. That at the 122, called *Le Boeuf à la Ficelle,* was named for a dish of beef tenderloin simmered in bouillon, a specialty of the house, which gained something from being served by waitresses naked except for high-heeled pumps and a camellia in their hair. The 122's kitchen also offered an omelet, although not for consumption. Instead, in a popular fetish, it was carried from the kitchen to a bedroom and there slid, hot and sizzling, onto the naked flesh of a client, with what effect one can only imagine.

It didn't take long for Paris to discover and adapt to the appetites of the American tourists who flooded into the city between the wars. Among the first to do so were the proprietors of Le Sphinx, a brothel in Montparnasse that opened in 1931. Instead of the system of payment operating in the larger *bordels,* where clients purchased *jetons* from the management and used them to recompense the girls, admission to Le Sphinx could be bought at the door. Clients passed through a lobby decorated with gilded sphinxes and sarcophagi into a mirrored cabaret where a band played *le jazz hot* for dancing and a *bar Americain* served the cocktails the French didn't drink. One visitor compared it to the first-class lounge of a transatlantic liner—except that, strolling among the tables and pausing occasionally to chat, were a number of attractive young women nude except for high-heeled shoes. If one wished to accompany one of them upstairs and become better acquainted, the management spoke most languages and accepted all currencies. Otherwise, one drank one's martini, listened to the band and admired the view.

The superficial elegance of the brothel culture hid a punishing regime. Women were expected to service a minimum of four men a day. As food and lodging were deducted from their earnings, most were deeply in debt. Occasionally a woman bought herself out but in general their future was bleak. Beating or even mutilating a prostitute was considered a misdemeanor at most. Science confirmed their physical and intellectual inferiority. A textbook of the time asserted that, "What the criminal is to men, the prostitute is to women." It also concluded that the skulls of prostitutes—and therefore their brains—were smaller than those of ordinary women, so however attractive as sex objects, they had no more standing as sentient beings than a lap dog.

Grandes Horizontales

The liberality of the *belle époque* permitted women who, a few generations before, had been ostracized as prostitutes, to rebrand themselves as *poules de luxe, courtisanes* or, more colloquially, *grandes horizontales*; i.e., women who distinguish themselves on their backs. They had no need to work in brothels. Instead they had clients or "protectors" who took care of their material needs. Men-about-Paris competed to share the latest beauties, just as they schemed to acquire the newest thoroughbred horse or most elegantly caparisoned carriage. Among these women, to maintain just the right degree of notoriety became an art. In René Clair's witty period comedy *The Flame of New Orleans*, a *roué* from Europe is startled to see Marlene Dietrich plying her trade so far from her native Paris. Asked by a friend "Did you know her?", he replies, "I didn't *know* her exactly. But I know *stories about* her."

Popular culture loved such people. Women in particular admired them. They demonstrated that beauty and intelligence could help one win in a man's world. Verdi's *La Traviata* was inspired by Marie Duplessis, who juggled half a dozen lovers at a time. (She allocated one night a week to each. They collaborated to buy a bureau with enough drawers for each to have a change of clothes.) Among them was Alexandre Dumas *fils,* who wrote the novel *La Dame aux Camellias* on which the opera was based.

A few dramatists, such as Émile Augier, tried to present such women as evil and depraved. The main character of his *Mariage d'Olympe* is weighed down by guilt, the husband and not the lover is the hero of his marital triangle drama *Gabrielle,* while in his libretto for Charles Gounod's opera *Sapho,* the Greek poet isn't a lesbian at all, but labeled as such by a jealous rival. All these are forgotten today, while such celebrations of the self-indulgent society as Franz Lehar's operetta *The Merry Widow* have never been off stage. In this joyously decadent romance, the libertine Count Danilo is recruited to lure back from Paris the richest woman in his principality who has moved there, with her fortune. Through a tortuous

The Merry Widow, 1934

set of circumstances of the kind that only happen in bedroom farces, he mistakes her for a prostitute and spends the rest of the story repairing his gaffe.

Initially a flop, *The Merry Widow* took off when one of its locales was changed to Maxim's, the Parisian restaurant famed for the beauty of the women who congregated there. The change transformed call girls into figures of glamor and Danilo from a cynical sensualist into a hero of love and the good life. The best-known version, Ernst Lubitsch's 1934 film, starring real-life Lothario Maurice Chevalier, celebrates a culture where the women have no last names and no relationship lasts more than a night. The lyrics of one of the show's most popular tunes spell it out:

At Maxim's once again

I swim in pink champagne

When people asks what bliss is

I simply answer, "*This* is!"

Lolo, Dodo, JouJou

CloClo, Margot, FrouFrou!

Since surnames do not matter

I take the first to hand.

Maxim's lived up to its legend. When the restaurant was sold in 1932, the new owners decided to install air conditioning and better lighting. According to cultural historian Joseph Wechsberg, "when they pushed away the red plush banquettes, they exposed heaps of jewelry, gold coins and garters that had been lost in the long wild nights."

Les Règles de Jeux

Sexology is not a field in which the French traditionally excel. Germans and Austrians pioneered serious research. *Psychopathia*

Sexualis by Richard von Krafft-Ebing, published in 1886, introduced the terms "masochism," after the erotic writer and sensualist Leopold von Sacher-Masoch, author of *Venus in Furs*, and "sadism," for the Marquis de Sade. Magnus Hirschfeld's Institut für Sexualwissenschaft in Berlin defined fetishism, while Sigmund Freud in Vienna pioneered an understanding of human behavior's sexual foundation. The torch then passed to the American Alfred Kinsey who, with a number of collaborators, compiled *Sexual Behavior in the Human Male* (1948) and *Sexual Behavior in the Human Female* (1953).

Most French research has been left to amateurs, among them novelist and art historian Henri-Pierre Roché (featured later in this book) and writer André Breton. Breton's attempt to analyze the sexual tastes and habits of his fellow Surrealists would barely rate a footnote, except for the bemused way he confronted the results, which says much about the nature of French sexuality behind the veil of sophistication and romance.

Surrealism grew out of the First World War. Breton, working in a psychiatric hospital, noticed how some patients, despite having little education, invented elaborate fantasies to rationalize their experiences. One believed that trench warfare was a huge show, organized from behind the scenes, with fake explosions, and bodies supplied by mortuaries. From where did such ideas emerge? Breton intuited that our unconscious was a reservoir of creativity, tapped only at times of stress, or while dreaming, or in a hypnotic trance. He determined to explore this capacity using dreams, games, and surveys like one he conducted about the sex lives of the poets, painters and film-makers who made up the Surrealist group.

Twelve sessions took place between 1928 and 1932, and primarily involved Paul Éluard, Max Ernst, Raymond Queneau, Jacques Prévert, Benjamin Péret, Pierre Unik, Luis Buñuel and Breton himself. Topics included sexual practice: how often, how much, with whom, in what locations (bed, bath, the open), dressed or naked: the sexual imagination—fantasies during sex and masturbation, pornography, sex talk, lingerie: female anatomy—the clitoris; the relative attractiveness of shaved vs. natural pubic hair, etc.

As well as numerous girlfriends and models, such fellow travellers of the group as Gala Éluard, Meret Oppenheim, Jeanne Buñuel, Georgette Magritte, Maria Vassilieff, Nina Hamnett and Elsa Triolet would surely have had something to say on the subject, but it wasn't until the ninth session that women took part and their input was negligible. For all its apparent enlightenment, Surrealism remained, like so much else in the business of sex, a boys' club.

Some of the all-male discussions were almost comically technical, such as this from Session 11 with Breton, Albert Valentin, Paul Éluard, Pierre Unik and Georges Sadoul.

Breton: "Valentin, what do you think of the idea of masturbating and coming in a woman's ear?"

Valentin: "I wouldn't dream of it!"

Éluard: "I've already done it. It's very good . . .No, *not* very good . . . It depends."

Sadoul: "I've never done it, but it appeals to me."

Breton: "It would only satisfy one side of the woman [i.e., could only be done in one ear at a time]. These things aren't very well organized."

Unik: "The ear is made for the tongue, not for the cock."

Sadoul (thoughtfully): "What about in the nose?"

Breton instigated the discussions in the wake of having been thrown over by his lover Suzanne Muzard, inspiration for the eponymous main character of his one novel, *Nadja*. Why he might have been an inadequate lover was suggested in the first session, when Queneau posed the general question, "Do you always make love in the same way? If not, are the variations in order to increase your own pleasure or that of the woman?"

Péret, Prévert and Unik all agreed that the woman's pleasure was paramount. "Like Péret," Unik said, "I always ask the woman what she prefers."

But Breton was astonished. "I find that absolutely extraordinary, quite phenomenal. Talk about complications!"

All Good Americans . . .

The first Americans to visit Paris *en masse* arrived after the First World War. Before then, the few visitors belonged to one of three categories: the very rich, the very poor, or those with something to hide.

The rich had been coming to France for a century. They bought houses from which to embark on the Grand Tour, raced horses, collected art, and relaxed in its restaurants, clubs and brothels. Brides-to-be traditionally had their wedding dresses made in Paris by Poiret or Worth, assembled their *trousseaux* there, bought silver and porcelain, and acquired a French maid or cook. In the late 19th century it became fashionable to marry into aristocracy. Henry James and Edith Wharton amusingly and sometimes resignedly documented the annual invasion of heiresses, eager for a title.

The poor headed for Paris because money lasted longer there than in any other civilized city. As Ernest Hemingway gloated in his first dispatch after arriving in 1921, one could live for a year on a thousand dollars, and Scott Fitzgerald marveled that a four-course meal, with wine, was available for the equivalent of 18 *cents*. And if age, illness or a suicidal inclination gave you not long to live, how much sweeter to die in the arms of a French lover to the sound of an accordion playing *La Vie en Rose*.

The third group—those for whom Paris was a place to hide—cut across the classes. It included "remittance men," sent there by their families after some particularly reprehensible behavior, and paid to stay away. There was little one couldn't do in Paris, providing one was discreet. Prostitution, homosexuality and interracial relationships were legal, and drug use unrestricted. Nor did France forbid the publication and sale of pornography—providing it was written in a language other than French.

Gertrude Stein and Natalie Clifford Barney were typical of monied Americans who found Paris a congenial place to live as both lesbians and intellectuals, neither regarded as appropriate for women on the other side of the Atlantic. Lesbianism and cross-dressing flourished in such clubs as Le Monocle, which opened in Montparnasse in the 1920s and remained a social center for the richer end of the lesbian community until World War II. It required clients to wear evening dress. Women were admitted in gowns, providing their companions dressed in male black tie, ideally with a monocle.

World War I made narcotics more commonplace in Europe. In London, "ladies" attended "morphine teas" where, after being served their *lapsang souchong,* the servants were dismissed and guests rolled up their sleeves for the injection of the drug. Harrod's, the city's most exclusive department store, marketed a range of morphine gels and cocaine, with a syringe, in a chic leather wallet, as a gift for loved ones in the trenches. In Paris, cocaine, morphine and heroin could be bought at pharmacies (although aspirin, a synthetic, and therefore suspect, required a prescription). The purses of many fashionable women contained a Pravaz, the preferred brand of hypodermic. (It was also available in silver, and inlaid with precious stones, as an elegant gift.) Cannabis was sold as resin (*hashish*) or mixed with tobacco. Opium dissolved in alcohol as laudanum was the Prozac of the day, while the smokable variety was freely available at such *fumeries* or "opium dens" as Paris's Drosso's.

Celebrities who might have been expected to set a good example to their compatriots often behaved worse than anyone. Scott and Zelda Fitzgerald rioted through clubs and cabarets from Montmartre to Antibes, on one occasion kidnapping the musicians from a café and locking them all night in a basement. Novelist Ford Madox Ford grew so weary of his home being trashed that he held his parties in one of the public dance halls known as *bals musettes*, preferring that his less inhibited guests wreck its furniture rather than his own.

San Francisco-born Isadora Duncan led the émigré community in extravagance. A pioneer of modern dance, she partied, as she performed, in a minimum of clothing. Novelist Michel Georges-Michel described her reclining on a couch, Roman fashion, where she "poured out champagne from an immense amphora of jade to all those who reached up with their cups. She let down her hair, loosened her clothing, and asked everybody to follow her example. 'It is as indecent to be dressed when the company is nude as to be sober when everybody is drunk.'" Duncan died violently in 1927, yanked by the neck onto a street in Nice as her trailing scarf caught in a wheel of the car rushing her to the bed of a new lover. She could not have wished for a better end.

All these people, as well as those Hemingway called "ladies of all sexes," met and mixed freely with tourists and the curious at such watering holes as the Café du Dôme in Montparnasse. A writer for *The New Yorker* luxuriated in its promiscuous variety. "The Dôme blossoms like some impossible mushroom. Tables huddle together in a vast mélange and spill into the street, where the shifting mob laugh, whistle, gesticulate, consume vast quantities of aperitifs and liqueurs, and vociferously absolve themselves of America. It's not true that the Dôme is solely occupied by transatlantic wastrels and pretenders. There are ambitious young poets here, aspiring musicians, intense experimenters in creative prose. Why they are here is unexplainable. The Dôme offers nothing but a churning oasis of the Left Bank where Americans may see one another and, gratified with the spectacle of kindred blood in a foreign land, succumb to the delectable illusion that they are liberated."

Among Friends

One French word at least resisted the almost universal acceptance of "Latin terms." In 1925, Jean Galtier-Boissière, creator of the satirical periodical *Le Crapouillot,* wrote, "The upper classes have invented a new vice. All these blasé individuals no longer take great pleasure in doing what you think; the greater pleasure, for them, is watching each other do it. We call it '*La Partouze*'!"

"Group sex," "swinging," and "orgy" have had some currency, but nobody has yet found a more elegant term for what one definition calls "a party during which the participants (whose number generally exceeds four) practice the exchange of partners and engage in collective and simultaneous sexual activities." The name is particularly applicable when such activities are pursued with special attention to the location, the rules of behavior and the choice of participants.

Serious *partousiers* distinguish between the semi-public sex of *échangiste* or *libertin* clubs, where people arrive as couples or individuals, without invitation, and require only the price of admission, and the more social *partouze,* where no money changes hands, participants generally know one another or have been introduced by a member, and an agreed etiquette prevails. For example, to have sex outside the circle with someone met there is frowned on: what takes place in the *partouze* stays there. Also, if couples participate, they must discard any *bourgeois* prejudices with their clothes: for the period of the *partouze,* sex transcends religion, race, class and the bonds of marriage. For at least one of the relationships described in this book, the introduction of jealousy to the equation proved toxic.

La partouze was not, any more than the connoisseurship of food, a French invention, but France can claim, as in that case, to have refined it, laid down rules for its pursuit, and written about it in a way that encourages other countries to explore and vary it according to local tastes and customs. As one of the most active *partousieurs* of recent times put it, surely sex is sufficiently serious to deserve at least the respect accorded a canvas by Picasso or a Fauré *pavane*—if not, some might say, even more.

~ ❖ ~

The essays that follow describe some of the ways men and women have used their lives to define and enlarge the concept of Love. That all did so, at least in part, in Paris was no coincidence. As blatantly as if it hung out a sign, the city has advertised itself as a venue for the exploration of passion in all its forms and its capacity for exaltation and despair. As James Joyce is supposed to have said (although the source is obscure), "Paris is a lamp for lovers hung in the wood of the world"—but, to pursue that analogy, a lamp can light our way but also lure us further into that darkness where what Baudelaire called *les fleurs de mal*—the flowers of evil— bloom. Even in the saddest of these stories, however, there always remains that most poignant of epitaphs—"I remember, once . . . in Paris . . . "

Chapter 1.

LOVE IMPERIAL: NAPOLÉON BONAPARTE AND JOSÉPHINE DE BEAUHARNAIS

As with most military and political leaders, Napoléon Bonaparte found his greatest satisfaction in power. No other sensation could compete. He was fortunate, however, to encounter, in Joséphine de Beauharnais, a woman able to override his military and political preoccupations and introduce him to the pleasures of the flesh.

Marie Josèphe Rose Tascher de La Pagerie never expected to be empress of France. Nothing in her origins even hinted at it. She came to France as a teenager from the Caribbean island of Martinique to enter an arranged marriage with Alexandre de Beauharnais, a spendthrift and womanizer. They had two sons before the 1789 revolution took his life and imprisoned her for a year.

In post-revolutionary France, governed by a committee called the *Directoire* or Directorate, she lived by her wits, eventually drifting into the orbit of powerbroker and *Directoire* member Paul Barras. A homosexual, Barras, according to an admirer, "surrounded himself with beautiful and witty women whom he never touched," but who were useful in influencing men to fall in with his plans. Marie Josèphe became one of them.

Of the five *Directoire* members, Barras alone would survive to the end of its regime, only to be supplanted, ironically, by his own protegé, Napoléon Bonaparte. Among the first to recognize the talents of the young artilleryman, Barras called on him in 1793 when the British attempted to invade a weakened France through the port of Toulon. He used him again in 1795 to disperse angry royalists who filled the streets of Paris. Instead of sending in troops, Bonaparte used cannons to obliterate them and their barricades with, as one admirer put it, "a whiff of grapeshot." In appreciation, Barras made him military governor of the city.

Seeing the value of having an ally in Bonaparte's bed, Barras encouraged a romance between the young general and Marie Josèphe de Beauharnais. Both had much to gain from such a union. The unworldly Napoléon, though a military genius, was still a Corsican provincial; poor, socially inept, with a gaggle of relatives to support. As for Marie Josèphe, a widow with two children and a dubious reputation, she was burdened with expensive tastes but with no fortune to finance them. She was also showing her 39 years. "She is small and has a pretty, delicate stature," wrote a contemporary. "Her face must have been pleasant [once], and [still] gives an air of understanding as well as finesse. Nonetheless, she has a face of a woman of the world; one with a certain amount of experience. Her complexion is yellow." Like many women of the time, she also had bad teeth, most of which had gone black. Because of this, she never smiled.

Josephine signing the act of her divorce, by E.M. Ward, 1853

When Barras introduced them at a reception, Napoléon was more attracted to another of his "stable," Thérése Tallien. Fortunately chance provided a second opportunity. As military governor, Napoléon prohibited Parisians from keeping weapons in their homes. Any found were seized, including a sword that had belonged to Marie Josèphe's late husband. Her son, Eugène, then 14, asked to have it back for sentimental reasons, and Napoléon, impressed with his courage, agreed. Marie Josèphe visited to thank him in person. Within a few days they were inseparable, and Napoléon was using the pet name by which she became famous—Joséphine.

He proposed in January 1796 and they married in March but, as the Duke of Wellington said of the battle of Waterloo, "it was a damned close-run thing." The ceremony was set for 8 p.m., but while the bride, notary and witnesses, including Barras, arrived early, the groom did not. Everyone except Joséphine went home.

Napoléon appeared, unapologetic, at 10 p.m., having gotten side-tracked examining some military maps.

A lifetime army man, accustomed to being obeyed without question, he never adjusted to domesticity. He would demand a hot bath at 2 a.m. and meals at all hours, which he ate randomly; sometimes dessert first, and meat at the end: "It all ends up in the same place," he rationalized. Joséphine also struggled with the fact that she didn't love him. "I find myself in a state of lukewarmness that I dislike," she wrote a friend. It was less of a problem than it would be today, when a degree of affection is expected, even demanded in marriage, whereas 19th century unions put money and status first. Companionability was a bonus, attraction a gift, indifference the norm.

Joséphine decided that, if she couldn't make the general a gentleman, she could at least domesticate him by sharing her sexual experience. He was soon entranced. "Without his Joséphine," he wailed in one of his numerous letters, "without the assurance of her love, what is left him upon earth? What can he do?" Writing from the battlefield, he pleaded, "I shall be alone and far, far away. But you are coming, aren't you? You are going to be here beside me, in my arms, on my breast, on my mouth? Take wing and come, come." He didn't disguise what he enjoyed most about their relationship. "A kiss on your heart," one letter concluded, "and one much lower down. *Much* lower!" The smell of her body particularly enticed him, the gamier the better. "Do not wash!" ordered one note, "I am coming."

With Napoléon often absent at the head of his army, Joséphine, bored, drifted back to Barras and his circle. Uninhibited and still voluptuous, she became one of the *Incroyables et Merveilleuses*—Incredible and Wonderful Ones, also known as the Celestials, who modeled the most outrageous new gowns. France had a flourishing silk weaving industry, and since silk, as a wit observed, "was invented so that women could go naked while clothed," *couturiers* indulged themselves with imitations of Greek and Roman clothing at their flimsiest. A cartoon by British satirist Gillray showed Joséphine and Thérése Tallien dancing naked for Barras. He's too drunk to take any notice but an eager Napoléon has crept in and is sneaking a look.

Pining, Napoléon begged Joséphine to join him at the front. Having made his headquarters in Milan, he was furious that she was having too much fun in Paris to make the long and dangerous journey. His letter is drenched in self-pity. "I arrive in Milan. I rush to your apartment. I left everything to see you, to hug you . . . You weren't there. You enchant cities with parties, yet you move away from me when I arrive. You no longer care about your dear Napoléon. A whim made you love him, inconstancy makes you indifferent. Do not bother; pursue pleasures; happiness is for you. The whole world is happy if you desire it so, but your husband is alone and very, very unhappy."

Back in Paris, he built her a chateau at Malmaison on the outskirts of the city with an estate within which she created a famous rose garden and assembled a private zoo, importing animals from around the world. Ostriches, emus, seals, zebras, gazelles, antelopes, llamas, black swans and even kangaroos roamed free on its grounds and in its lakes and streams. Napoléon didn't take her menagerie seriously, and on his occasional visits surreptitiously fed tobacco to the antelopes and gazelles. The nicotine made them frisky and they chased her maids, to their consternation and his amusement.

In 1798, having conquered Egypt, Napoléon returned to Paris where, as he put it, "I found the crown of France lying in the gutter." In a *coup d'etat*, he overturned the enfeebled *Directoire* to become Emperor. At his coronation in Notre Dame, as Pope Pius VII prepared to place the crown on his head, he impulsively took it and crowned himself, then Joséphine, a signal that domination of the French state by Rome and the Catholic church was at an end.

Anxious to establish a dynasty, Napoléon concentrated on producing an heir, but without success. Since Joséphine had already borne children, he assumed the fault was his—until, in 1807, while campaigning in Poland, he met 21-year-old countess Marie Walewska at a ball given in his honor. At noon the next day, a coach stopped in front of the Walewski mansion. Grand Marshal Duroc descended, carrying a gigantic bouquet of flowers and a letter. Signed simply "N," it read "I have seen only you, I have admired only you, I desire only you." As Poland desperately needed Napoléon's protection from its larger neighbors, in particular Russia, the 70-year-old count was persuaded to surrender his wife for the good of the state. Marie and Napoléon became lovers, and in 1810 she presented him with a son, Alexandre.

Being illegitimate, the child couldn't inherit, but with this proof that the failure to produce a heir lay with Joséphine, his advisors urged Napoléon to divorce her and take a new, younger wife, ideally with a pedigree appropriate to a future ruler of Europe. His love for Joséphine seems never to have faltered but his dynastic longings were stronger. A hurried search among suitable consorts settled on Princess Marie-Louise of Austria, and he reluctantly informed Joséphine of his decision. Instead of a divorce, their marriage was annulled on the technicality that they hadn't confirmed the civil wedding with a religious one.

Paintings depicting the renunciation generally show Joséphine as a tragic heroine, slumped in a chair, weeping, while Napoléon either ineffectually holds her hand or makes his escape. In fact, she gave more thought to the financial arrangements for their separation, which were generous. He agreed to keep her in the style to which she had become accustomed, even offering to let her retain the title of empress. She accepted the money but declined the honor, preferring the family name of her first husband. For the rest of her life, she was simply Joséphine de Beauharnais.

Napoleon married Marie Louise on 11 March, 1810. Rather than waste time travelling to Vienna, he let her uncle say "I do" on his behalf. The bride left for Paris immediately after the ceremony, and though the couple had barely met, she was soon pregnant. "I bought a womb," Napoléon joked. But it was a poor investment. Their son inherited the chronically poor health of the in-bred Hapsburgs. Despite his proud father calling him *L'Aiglon,* the Young Eagle, and loading him with titles—he was King of Rome, Napoléon II and Duke of Reichstadt—the boy was sickly from the start, and died at 21.

Joséphine, though no longer empress, continued to spend like one. She expanded the gardens at Malmaison, building new hothouses, as well as commissioning hundreds of dresses and quantities of jewelry. On six occasions following their divorce, the state had to rescue her from bankruptcy. Before she died in 1814 at the age of 51, maintaining her life-style had cost more than thirty million francs.

Also in 1814, Napoléon, defeated by Nelson at Trafalgar, Wellington in Spain, and the winter in Russia, was forced to abdicate and accept exile on Elba, a tiny Mediterranean island. He still clung to the illusion of his legacy, even though Marie-Louise had taken a lover and he would never see her or his son again. Marie Walewska joined him, bringing their child in hopes he would renounce imperial ambitions and settle down with her. Napoléon refused.

In 1815 he escaped from Elba, raised an army, and confronted the combined European forces at Waterloo in Belgium. This time, the British took no chances with their defeated enemy, imprisoning him on the Atlantic island of St. Helena, one of the remotest spots on earth. He died there in May 1871, still in exile. His last words were of battles won and of the woman who showed him there was more to life than war: *"La France*

... *l'armée* ... *tête d'armée* ... *Joséphine*" ("France ... the army ... head of the army ... Joséphine".)

~❖~

Footnote. After Waterloo, Napoléon, with the agreement of President James Madison, planned to spend the rest of his life in the United States. American ships were ready to spirit him away but the British learned of the plan and kept him at sea until he could be conveyed to St. Helena.

Chapter 2.

UNHEALTHY RELATIONS: GEORGE SAND AND ALFRED DE MUSSET

I n 1833, a cheaply produced, blisteringly erotic and sacrilegious novella called *Gamiani or Two Nights of Excess* caused a sensation in Paris. Supposedly the memoir of "Baron Alcide de Mxxx," it described how a young man, enchanted by the beautiful but mysterious Italian Countess Gamiani, hides in her bedroom after a ball. From a dressing room, he watches her initiate a girl into the pleasures of lesbian sex until, aroused past endurance, he bursts out of his hiding place and joins them in bed. For the rest of the night, the three indulge themselves, resting between bouts of activity by describing their erotic adventures, including bestiality with a donkey and an orangutan, an encounter with flagellating monks and an orgy with an order of nuns. Gamiani's maid and a large dog join the proceedings, which conclude with the countess poisoning the girl and then herself, in the hope that "there might be the possibility of pleasure in the extreme of pain."

Drawing of George Sand,
by Alfred de Musset, 1833

Gamiani became the most widely read and reprinted erotic work of the 19th century, running to more than 40 editions. Few people suspected its author was one of France's most respected young poets and novelists, Alfred de Musset, and its inspiration the even more prominent Amandine Aurore Lucie Dupin, Baroness Dudevant, better known as George Sand.

As a catalog of depravity, *Gamiani* rivaled the works that sent the Marquis de Sade to imprisonment in the Bastille. The risk Musset ran in publishing it suggests the intensity of his passion. Its libels of the church alone were more than enough to have him jailed.

The 23-year-old poet was an unlikely pornographer. Handsome, soft-featured and dreamy, he accentuated an air of weary sensitivity by wearing pink suits, which contrasted with his red beard and moustache as well as showing up his pallor.

Sand could not have been more different. Just under five feet tall, she scandalized even bohemian Paris by wearing male suits, top hats and heavy boots, sporting a cane and smoking a pipe. Cross-dressing made it easier to prowl the slums in search of material for her writing, but she came to prefer male clothes to the corsets and crinolines of a respectable *bourgeoise*.

Notwithstanding having a husband and children, she shared her bed with lovers of both sexes. Her affair with Musset began with a series of passionate letters in which he stammered out his love while sneaking his fantasies about her into *Gamiani*. It was a time for such emotional excess. The great writers of Europe's Romantic Age, Byron, Shelley and Keats, had been dead for about a decade but their influence was undiminished. All had been swept up in the frenzy of France's 1789 revolution and the rise of Bonaparte, only to see him fall, leaving them haunted with a sense of life's brevity and the need to fill it with sensation. Byron would write:

For the sword outwears its sheath

And the soul wears out the breast

And the heart must pause to breathe

And love itself have rest.

Shelley complained,

Alas! I have nor hope nor health

Nor peace within nor calm around . . .

I could lie down like a tired child

And weep away the life of care.

John Keats wrote of being half in love with easeful death," a sentiment echoed by Musset.

Keats, Shelley and Musset all suffered from tuberculosis, considered at the time an illness peculiar to creative people. A sense of their imminent demise was also believed to increase sexual desire and confer extraordinary powers of seduction on its sufferers. Awareness of his mortality drove Musset to sample all the physical sensations. "I cannot help myself," he wrote. "Infinity torments me." At 15, on one of his first visits to a prostitute, he contracted syphilis, the tremors of which became more evident as he aged. In response, he drank absinthe and smoked opium. They induced "out of body" experiences in which he imagined he was watching himself as another person.

As had been the case with Byron, whose reputation as "mad, bad and dangerous to know" just increased his allure, Musset's addictions encouraged women to comfort and pleasure him. This may have influenced Sand's decision to join him on a holiday in Venice in 1834, an acceptance she soon had reason to regret, since she contracted dysentery in the two weeks it took to get there. Things began to look up when Pietro Pagello, the doctor summoned by their Venetian hotel, turned out to be young and handsome. Physician and patient felt an immediate rapport, which increased as Musset neglected Sand to explore the city and its pleasures. When he caught dysentery himself and Pagello was again called, he had to watch helplessly as she and the young doctor flirted at his bedside.

Sand sent Musset back to Paris alone. By the time she returned with Pagello six months later, the whole city knew their story, or at least Musset's version of it, and condemned Sand's behavior. When Pagello went back to Italy in October, Musset, who had continued to barrage Sand with recriminatory letters, chose the moment to announce he no longer loved her. This precipitated a last-ditch gesture of reconciliation. In November he received a parcel. Inside was her luxuriant hair, which she had cut off as proof of her devotion. He burst into tears at the extravagance of the gesture, and by January they were reconciled. The reunion didn't last, however, and they parted definitively in March of 1835.

At the same time, Sand decided to divorce her free-spending husband. The lawyer she hired to represent her, Michel de Bourges, was not as handsome as Pagello nor as creative as Musset, but perhaps that was the attraction. Their relationship continued until Sand met the man with whom her name would always be most associated.

Polish pianist and composer Frédéric Chopin, yet another victim of tuberculosis, was not initially impressed with her. After the party at which they met, he observed to a friend, "What an unattractive person *la Sand* is. Is she really a woman?" But her brilliance overwhelmed him as it had so many others. Once they became lovers, Sand peremptorily decided Chopin's health demanded he leave Paris, and transported him to the Spanish island of Majorca. The holiday rivaled in misadventure her Venetian vacation with Musset. The weather was cold and wet, which exacerbated Chopin's illness. He couldn't compose on the available pianos so his own instrument had to be shipped from Paris, at great expense and inconvenience. Pious locals disapproved of the couple not attending mass on Sunday and ostracized them once they discovered they were not married. On their return to France, Sand wrote to a friend, "One more month and we would die in Spain, Chopin and me; he with melancholy and disgust, I with anger and indignation. They hurt me in the most sensitive place of my heart, they pierced with pins a suffering being before my eyes. I will never forgive them and if I write about them, it will be with gall."

Chopin's health declined further and he died in 1849. He was only 39. Musset survived him only until he turned 47. His relationship with Sand never revived but the verse he asked to be engraved on his tomb in Père Lachaise in 1857 suggests that he never forgot her:

Remember, when under the cold earth

My broken heart forever will sleep;

Remember, when the lonely flower

On my grave will gently open.

I will see you no more; but my immortal soul

Will come back to you like a faithful sister.

Listen, in the night,

A moaning voice:

Remember.

~ ❖ ~

Footnote. Musset's capacity to inspire the extravagant gesture survived his demise. In 1878, Henri Gervex devoted a canvas to his poem *Rolla,* showing its young hero taking one last look at his

beautiful mistress before jumping from a window to his death. The nude girl, sprawled across the bed, surrounded by lingerie—entangled with a riding crop—was too great an affront to the annual Salon, which refused to hang it.

Rolla, by Henri Gervex, 1878

Chapter 3.

DRUNK ON WORDS: ARTHUR RIMBAUD AND PAUL VERLAINE

Visitors to Paris who enter quiet, narrow rue Ferou, leading from the Luxembourg Gardens to stately Place St. Sulpice, are intrigued by text of a long poem painted on the wall that takes up one side of the street.

The poem is *Le Bateau Ivre (The Drunken Boat)* by Arthur Rimbaud. He recited it for the first time in 1871 in a room above a café on the far side of the square, now the Café de la Mairie. The poem describes how a boat whose crew has died makes its own delirious voyage to fantastic lands, including "incredible Floridas" inhabited by "panthers in the skins of men," before being wrecked and sinking into the depths. "I coiled through deeps of cloudless green," it continues in the vessel's voice, "Where, dimly, they come swaying down,/Rapt and sad, singly, the drowned . . . " and concludes with a repudiation of everything belonging to the society from which the writer emerged.

Beyond the brows of the seas,

I want none of Europe's waters unless it be

The cold black puddle where a child, full of sadness,

Squatting, looses a boat as frail

As a moth into the fragrant evening.

Rimbaud was only 17 when he wrote this, and had never left France, seen an ocean or been on any vessel larger than a rowboat. There was little poetry in Charleville, in the mountainous Ardennes, and even less in his impoverished childhood. His father, a soldier, returned home occasionally to impregnate his wife but, of his five children, was present for the birth of none. After the last, he just stopped coming back.

Arthur might have lived and died unknown. Fortunately, a teacher recognized his brilliance and encouraged him to read more widely and to study languages, including Latin, which he mastered with ease. He began writing poetry at 15, inspired by Charles Baudelaire, whose work celebrated the "artificial paradises" accessible through the use of opium and other drugs. To Rimbaud he was "the first seer, king of poets, a true God." Reading Baudelaire convinced him that great poetry required a "long, immense and reasoned disorder of all the senses." Only by "absorbing all the poisons and keeping only the quintessences" could one achieve an insight into the unknown.

Baudelaire also sparked the imagination of Paul Verlaine, who had just published his first poems in Paris. He was ten years older than Rimbaud and came from a prosperous but conventional family that pushed him into marrying and taking a respectable office job. With such contrasting backgrounds, it's unlikely the two men would ever have met had it not been for the events of 1871.

Following France's defeat in the Franco-Prussian war, the siege of Paris by the Prussians and the fall of Emperor Louis-Napoléon,

Paul Verlaine and Arthur Rimbaud (seated, at left), in
Henri Fantin-Latour's *By the Table*, from 1872

the capital became, briefly, an open city, controlled by a volun-
teer National Guard and a group of idealistic anarchists; a period
known as the Commune. Elated by the prospect of social change,
Rimbaud dropped out of school and visited Paris for the first
time. He met publishers and editors but none offered him work,
although one suggested he contact Verlaine, who led a group of
writers called *Les Vilains Bonshommes* or The Disreputables.

Back in Charleville, Rimbaud began corresponding with Verlaine,
who urged him to return to Paris, and sent him a train ticket. "Come,
dear great soul," he wrote, "we are calling you, we are waiting for
you!" This was all the encouragement Rimbaud needed.

He lived for a time with Verlaine and his 19-year-old wife, but
Mathilde Verlaine, who had just given birth to their first child, dis-
liked the surly teenager with uncombed hair and a corncob pipe
permanently clamped between his teeth. She was glad when he

moved out, as she had also noticed a growing affection between the two men that went beyond simple friendship.

After the reading of *Le Bateau Ivre, Les Vilains Bonshommes* invited Rimbaud to join, but soon regretted doing so, since he became violent when drunk, stabbing even Verlaine during an argument, and attacking another man with a sword cane. A portrait of the group by Henri Fantin-Latour captured the unease he created. One member refused outright to appear on the same canvas. A vase of flowers replaced him. Of the rest, none is looking at any of the others, with the exception of Rimbaud, who stares raptly at Verlaine, the two isolated off to one side, as if shunned by the group.

Verlaine found Rimbaud a room in Montmartre where they would meet in secret. As their friendship turned into a love affair, his marriage reached crisis. He and Mathilde argued until they came to blows. In July 1872, feeling ill, she asked Verlaine to fetch a doctor. He did so, but instead of returning home, went to Rimbaud, who said, "I was going to your house to tell you. I've decided to leave Paris." Verlaine protested, begging for time to settle things with Mathilde. "Forget your wife," Rimbaud said. "I tell you we're leaving. Are you coming or not?"

Unable to bear the thought of losing the boy he had come to call his "infernal husband," Verlaine never returned home nor saw his wife or child again. Instead he and Rimbaud took a train to Belgium. After stopping briefly in Brussels, they crossed the channel to London, where they scraped a living giving French lessons. Drunk most of the time, they fought until Verlaine decided to return to Paris. He resolved to patch things up with Mathilde, but if she refused, to shoot himself.

He got as far as Brussels, where Rimbaud caught up with him, and the arguments escalated. On July 10, 1873, Verlaine shot Rimbaud twice, one bullet lodging in his wrist. The police were called and though Rimbaud didn't press charges, a judge decided Verlaine was the villain of the event. Labeling him a pederast who had corrupted an innocent teenager, he jailed him for two years.

Rimbaud returned to Charleville and worked on two prose poems that posterity would regard as his finest work, *Illuminations* and *A Season in Hell.* They reflect a search for the transcendence others found in love or religion. "I managed to make every trace of human hope vanish from my mind," he wrote. "I pounced on every joy like a ferocious animal, eager to strangle it."

Verlaine was released six months early for good behavior, and the lovers met briefly in Brussels. Rimbaud entrusted to Verlaine the manuscripts of both *Illuminations* and *A Season in Hell,* asking that he have them published. They never met again.

Verlaine's Catholic faith revived in prison but he found it of little use as he tried to pick up the threads of his life. Now divorced from Mathilde and alienated from his literary friends, he wrote some poetry and attempted to find publishers for Rimbaud's work, only to get drunk and burn most of the copies that were printed. Addicted to absinthe and suffering from diabetes and syphilis, he stumbled back each night from the cafés of Montparnasse to a rooming house on rue Descartes; the same building in which Ernest Hemingway would rent a room almost half a century later. Verlaine died there in 1896 at age 51. One of his last published works was devoted to poets he felt had not received their proper appreciation. He called the collection *Les Poètes Maudits (The Cursed Poets),* probably not realizing that the definition would apply equally to him.

Rimbaud drifted to Cyprus, then to North Africa, where he spent the rest of his life as a merchant, involved in a succession of schemes, including gunrunning. Meanwhile, in France, both his poetry and that of Verlaine were becoming famous. Every literature class would soon know Verlaine's *Autumn Song.*

The long sobs

Of the violins

Of autumn

Hurt my heart

With a monotonous languor.

In 1886, *Illuminations* and *Une Saison en Enfer* appeared in the magazine *La Vogue*. At the time, Rimbaud was crossing Ethiopia in charge of a caravan of 50 camels loaded with rifles. Did he still think of poetry? His letters suggest not. Rather, he felt he had gone beyond verse to an existence where words no longer had meaning. "It's exactly what I've always known," he wrote. "No more faith in history; principles forgotten. I'll stay silent. Envy me, poets and visionaries. I'm a thousand times richer, hoarding truth, like the sea."

~ ❖ ~

Footnote. During World War II, the BBC broadcast coded messages to the resistance in France. To warn that D-Day was imminent, they chose a verse of Verlaine. Baffled Nazi decoders struggled to untangle the military significance of *"Les sanglots longs des violons de l'automne blessent mon coeur d'une langueur monotone."*

Chapter 4.

LOVED I NOT HONOR MORE: GENERAL GEORGES BOULANGER AND MARGUERITE DE BONNEMAINS

In 1881, when the United States celebrated its centenary, a French guest at the ceremonies in Yorktown, Virginia, took exception to the German flag being flown next to the *tricolor*. The organizers intended it as a tribute to Baron Friedrich Wilhelm von Steuben, the military organizer who built Washington's army into an effective force, but the Frenchman pointed out that von Steuben did so as an employee of the French. It was they who selected him and sent him to America. The flag was hauled down, and honor, as General Georges Ernest Jean-Marie Boulanger saw it, restored.

Boulanger was the youngest general in the French army when he was appointed superintendent of the military school at St Cyr, France's West Point. No mere administrator but an effective agent of state power, he personally took command when the army was sent to crush a strike among miners, and settled the conflict without a shot being fired. Shortly after making a fuss at Yorktown, he became Director of the Infantry and, in 1886, when his school friend Georges Clemenceau was elected president, joined his cabinet as Minister of War. One of his first acts was to introduce a new and more efficient rifle for the army, but he won more friends by permitting all military officers for the first time to grow beards. Everyone from lieutenant upwards soon sported the same voluminous facial hair as himself. Though Clemenceau was ousted at the next election and Boulanger reverted to a serving officer, he was increasingly seen as a potential national figure.

The French army at the end of the 19th century was above public opinion or even civilian law. In 1894, a court martial found Captain Alfred Dreyfus guilty of espionage. The civil courts concurred, sending him to Devil's Island, even though many doubted the evidence that convicted him, attributing his conviction to a virulent national anti-Semitism. The real spy, a member of the military aristocracy, was soon exposed, but Dreyfus remained imprisoned until 1904, the army arguing that maintaining public confidence in its decisions mattered more than the freedom of an individual. Boulanger would probably have agreed, but by 1904 he was dead—and dead, to the astonishment of a nation that revered him, not for any military reason but out of love for a woman.

Boulanger's height, blue eyes and blonde beard and moustache commanded attention—of women in particular. Unhappily married and separated from his wife, he indulged in a number of affairs, none of them serious, until, in 1887, at a literary soirée, he met Marguerite, estranged wife of another cavalry officer, Pierre de Bonnemains. The dashing general and the frail, pale young woman

Suicide of General Boulanger at the cemetery
of Ixelles on the tomb of Marguerite,
Petit Journal, October 10, 1891

fell instantly in love, to the alarm of Boulanger's republican friends since, as well as being married, albeit separated, Marguerite came from a family of monarchists.

Boulanger saw no conflict in their relationship. As the poet Richard Lovelace put it, "I could not love thee (Dear) so much,/ Lov'd I not Honour more!" But his supporters were nervous, and strings were pulled to have him made head of the 13th Corps, stationed in Clermont-Ferrand, 400 kilometres from Paris. He took up the post in January 1888. Such was his popularity that a crowd gathered at the Gare de Lyon, trying to prevent the departure of his train. But any hopes that the lovers could be kept apart were thwarted. At Royat, a spa town near Clermont-Ferrand and conveniently connected to Paris by rail, a discreet establishment called *L'Auberge des Marronniers (The Inn of the Chestnut Trees)* welcomed couples who came supposedly to take the waters but actually to carry on affairs. As Marguerite suffered from tuberculosis, Royat's medicinal springs offered the perfect cover for the lovers to meet.

They managed four sojourns at this hideaway. Its owner, Marie Quinton, known as *La Belle Meuniere (The Beautiful Miller)*, filled their apartment with Marguerite's favorite red carnations and hired a special cook to prepare their meals. Experience had made her a shrewd observer of illicit relationships, and she foresaw a tragic end to this one if Marguerite wasn't ready to give up Boulanger to protect his career. "This man lives only for her," she wrote. "She will do with him what she wants. If she loves him for him more than for herself, she will make him great. Otherwise, all is lost."

Even absent from Paris, Boulanger's popularity increased, as did calls for his return. His enemies sent agents of the secret service, the Sûreté, to Clermont-Ferrand and discovered the lovers' stratagem. Recalled to Paris, he was placed under arrest on trumped-up charges of having plotted to overthrow the government. They also dismissed him from the army—a tactical error, since it left him free to run for office. In 1888 he was elected to the Chambre des Députés, France's Congress, to great jubilation. His speedy progress to the Elysée palace seemed just a matter of time.

Some urged that he follow Napoléon I by leading a coup, but Boulanger was too loyal to commit treason. His enemies then concocted a story that he was plotting such a *putsch* anyway, and had embezzled public funds to finance it. As a *député*, he was immune from prosecution, but honor was involved. He waived immunity and, to nobody's surprise except his own, was condemned by an administration intent on his downfall.

Distracted by Marguerite's declining health and with fears for their newborn child, Boulanger fled to Jersey, in the Channel Islands, before indictments could be handed down. He was sentenced in absentia to exile from France. Marguerite followed him to London and then Brussels, where Marie Quinton joined them as nurse and nanny, since Boulanger had decided to abandon politics and France altogether, and move to the United States.

Then Marguerite, who was only 39 but ravaged by tuberculosis, died in his arms on July 16, 1891. Boulanger was inconsolable. "I am nothing more than a body without a soul," he said. When she was buried at Ixelles near Brussels, he asked for the words *"À bientôt"* ("See you soon") to be engraved on her tombstone.

At 11:30 a.m. on Wednesday September 30, 1891, a carriage drawn by two horses stopped at the cemetery gate. Boulanger got out alone. Guards recognized him since he often came to lay red carnations on the grave. He walked to the slab under which Marguerite was buried, took a pistol from his pocket, put it to his head and fired. A suicide note found in his pocket asked that he be buried under the same stone as Marguerite, and that they add the words *"Ai-je bien pu vivre 2 mois et 1/2 sans toi!"* ("I could only live two and a half months without you!")

All France mourned the death of a man who had given up everything, even his life, for the woman he loved. Only his supposed friend, Georges Clemenceau, who had recruited him to politics, was unmoved. Chagrined at seeing a valuable ally destroy himself, and for something as trivial and abstract as love, he sneered, "He died as he lived—like a first lieutenant."

~❖~

Footnote. Marie Quinton kept a diary of her life as an innkeeper and the celebrities she met. *Diary of la Belle Meunière: General Boulanger and his Friend* was published in 1895 and became an instant bestseller. "Chance brought me close to General Boulanger at the most exciting period of his career," she wrote. "I saw up close, as I believe no one has been able to see, his private life, full of the superhuman love that embraced him to the point of suffocating him."

Chapter 5.

OBSESSION: ADÈLE HUGO AND ALBERT PINSON

"I dined yesterday at the Palais Royale," wrote novelist Honoré de Balzac in 1845. "Hugo's second daughter may be the greatest beauty I have seen in my life." Yet photographs of Adèle, daughter of the novelist Victor Hugo, tell a different story. "In the photos," observed a modern critic, "she always looks sad; devoured by a deep evil, haunted by a secret pain, inhabited by an intimate hell."

There wasn't much to do in the 1850s on the windswept island of Guernsey, just off the Brittany coast. The little social life took place in the mansions of a few wealthy exiles who chose to live there, almost in sight of the country that had disowned them. The most imposing of these residences was Hauteville House, home of Victor Hugo.

When emperor Louis-Napoléon condemned the author of *Notre Dame de Paris*—The Hunchback of Notre Dame—and *Les Misérables* to exile for questioning his illegal seizure of power, Hugo took his wife, daughter, two sons and mistress to Guernsey.

Adèle Hugo, c. 1856

Isolation increased the psychological distress of Adèle, recogniz-able today as the first stage of schizophrenia, a malady that had also afflicted her uncle. She never recovered from the trauma of losing her sister Leopoldine, who drowned, with her new husband, in an 1843 boating accident while on her honeymoon. After that, she was haunted by nightmares of death by water.

She also became convinced, with some justification, that her father loved her dead sister more than he did her, and resented Adèle's survival. He held spiritualist seances in hopes of com-municating with her spirit. Officers of the local British army garrison participated, among them Lieutenant Albert Andrew "Bertie" Pinson.

Pinson cut a handsome figure in the uniform of the 16th Regiment of Foot, set off by long moustaches, which he assiduously waxed and cultivated. Older then Adèle, he met her, probably not by chance, on the nearby island of Jersey in June 1854. "He saw me for the first time on a bench on the terrace in Jersey," she wrote in her diary. "I was absorbed in my book and I didn't see him. But he saw me, and from that day he loved me."

That Pinson felt anything for Adèle is doubtful. He could have modeled for the deceitful George Wickham of Jane Austen's *Pride and Prejudice* in his hopes of using a military career as a stepping stone to marrying money. Adèle's infatuation led to him becoming a regular dinner guest of the Hugos, sometimes several times a week. Hugo called him "a roughneck" and wrote that "his whole behavior is an enigma," but Adèle adored him. "I love you because you are English, royalist and blond," she wrote. "I don't expect to ignite your genius but I am satisfied to have melted the snow."

When Pinson proposed marriage, suggesting they move in England, she accepted eagerly, despite Hugo's disapproval. However, as the date of the wedding approached and Hugo showed no signs of warming to his potential son-in-law, Pinson concluded that the family fortune would always remain out of reach, and cut his losses. When Adèle and her mother arrived in London for the wedding, they found that Pinson and his regiment had departed for Halifax in the Canadian province of Nova Scotia.

Back on Guernsey, the jilted Adèle succumbed to delusions, depression, fever and stomach pains. The best therapy local doctors could suggest was to take up billiards, and also start smoking, tobacco being thought to have restorative powers. (Among its other therapeutic uses, puffing cigar smoke up the rectum was recommended to revive victims of drowning.) Hugo belittled her problems as mere hysteria but in 1858 sent her to Paris for treatment, from which she returned just as the emperor announced an amnesty for political exiles. Expecting that they'd now be moving back to Paris, Adèle collapsed when Hugo announced that, amnesty or not, he would never do so as long as Louis-Napoléon remained on the throne.

Shock and depression precipitated a decline in Adèle's mental state. After informing the family she was going to the Mediterranean island of Malta to convalesce, she instead crossed the Atlantic to Nova Scotia, determined to persuade or, if necessary, force Pinson into marriage. Finding that he hadn't wasted his few months in Halifax and was already engaged to a local girl, she put a pillow under her dress and called on his fiancée's father, claiming to be carrying Pinson's child. "You see the sufferings to which you expose me, by not marrying me?" she told him in a letter. "You send me to the battlefield of despair." To reassure him that she had money of her own and would also be the kind of wife who tolerated his extramarital diversions, she settled his gambling debts and even sent him a prostitute, paid for in advance. As a last resort, she hired a hypnotist in hopes that he could put him in a trance for as long as it took to marry her.

None of these stratagems worked, so when Adèle wrote to the family that she and Pinson had married at last, a suspicious Hugo demanded official confirmation. "The first concern of this son-in-law seems to be to make himself impossible," he fumed, "which he has managed to do. Is he, in fact, my son-in-law? His silence says no." Adèle's brother François-Victor confirmed his suspicions. "Adèle has deceived us as she deceived everyone," he wrote. "The marriage is not done." In a letter to Hugo, Pinson confirmed that he had definitely not married Adèle and had no intention of ever doing so.

Though he was undoubtedly a scoundrel, one can feel some sympathy for Pinson. Because of Adèle, the parents of his fiancée ended the engagement and sent her to Europe. When his regiment was posted to Barbados, in the West Indies, he hoped he'd finally escaped the increasingly disturbed young woman, but she followed him even there.

The disheveled woman had been seen walking the streets, still wearing her Canadian furs in the tropical heat. The residents of this remote Caribbean outpost were afraid of her. If she saw an English soldier, she accosted him, demanding news of Pinson in the French that few of them understood. A woman who rented her a house described her appearance. "She was a strange-looking person. She seemed to be wearing very dirty clothes, though fine. My saucy children said when she was gone they were glad I had given her a chair to sit on and not invited her on to the couch. Next evening the same person returned, accompanied by a young and fine-looking black woman, who spoke English well. She told me the lady's name was Madame Pinson [and] she was believed to be a daughter of Victor Hugo."

Adèle's new friend was Céline Alvarez Baa, who had seen the disheveled woman in the streets and taken pity on her. For the rest of her time there, she acted as her companion and translator, forced her to eat, and led her home when she was found wandering.

Like most schizophrenics, Adèle experienced periods of lucidity. During these, she wrote to her brothers, chatting about clothes, telling them she preferred the Caribbean climate to that of Nova Scotia and asking them to persuade their mother to pay her a visit. The French consul in Barbados wrote Hugo that "There is a mad woman here who calls herself your daughter" but her father was unmoved, agreeing to support Adèle only if she returned to France. "Let her come back," he wrote, "and at the same time as my heart blossoms, my arms will open."

In 1870, Pinson married the daughter of a lieutenant-colonel and left the army. Louis-Napoléon lost his throne in the Franco-Prussian War of 1871 and the Hugos moved back to Paris.

Adèle finally left Barbados in 1872, accompanied by Céline Baa, whom the Hugos paid to bring her back to France. Her former landlady recalled in a letter to her daughter that "your father, while passing the house, saw so much smoke he thought it was on fire. They were burning bedding, clothing, and various things too dirty to be packed up. When she left the house, the room she had occupied was inconceivably dirty. The floor was scrubbed twice, but we were finally obliged to take it up, the joists being quite destroyed."

The sea voyage restored some of Adèle's good looks and health but as she came down the gangplank from the steamer at St. Nazaire she gave no sign of recognizing her brothers who waited to welcome her. She never gave up her delusions. The rest of her life was passed in institutions, playing the piano and keeping a diary of her imaginary existence as Madame Pinson. Her father and brothers visited her from time to time. "She did not recognize François-Victor," Hugo wrote. "She recognized me. I embraced her. I spoke words of tenderness and hope to her. She was calm and seemed, sometimes, to be asleep."

Nothing more was heard of Bertie Pinson but for the rest of his life he must seldom have walked down any street without a glance over his shoulder.

~ ❖ ~

Footnote. Few people knew Adèle's story until François Truffaut filmed *L'Histoire d'Adèle H.* in 1975, shot in part on Guernsey, in the Hugo's former home. Twenty-year-old Isabelle Adjani gave an electric performance in her first screen role. "Adèle was mad, yes, probably," critic Roger Ebert wrote of the film, "but she lived her life on such a vast and romantic scale that it's just as well Pinson never married her. He would have been a disappointment."

Chapter 6

EVERYBODY OUGHT TO HAVE A MAID: CÉLESTE ALBARET AND MARCEL PROUST

"What I want to make clear is that I loved him," Céleste Albaret said of Marcel Proust. That she should speak with such emotion might seem surprising since she wasn't the social or intellectual equal of the author of *À la Recherche du Temps Perdu* but the housekeeper who cared for him during the last years of his life.

The French accept the possibility of love for one's god, country, wife, husband, lover, child, friend, even a pet. Seldom, however, is such intimacy conferred on a servant. For an employer to love a domestic or vice versa challenges the very structure of a society that celebrates liberty, equality and brotherhood but still at heart believes the classes are unequal.

For centuries, young women who aspired to more than the limited choices offered by the farm would head for the cities. Some married, others found jobs in shops or industry but many became *femmes de ménage;* maids of all work who did what all farm girls learned at their mothers' apron strings: cooking, cleaning, washing clothes, and caring for children.

Creative people and intellectuals, chronically preoccupied and impractical, relied on them. Without their help, the "Lost Generation" of expatriate writers could scarcely have survived. Gertrude Stein and Alice Toklas, despite the latter's skill in the kitchen, employed a succession of cooks. Ernest and Hadley Hemingway, even when they lived in an apartment without heating or running water, had a woman named Marie Rohrbach to cook, clean and look after their son, while Scott and Zelda Fitzgerald in Paris paid Lillian Maddock $26 a month as nanny for their daughter Scotty, congratulating themselves of having got a bargain: the going rate in New York was more than three times that.

Céleste Albaret

In 1923, 22-year-old Augustine Célestine Gineste, known as Céleste, left a village near the southern city of Montpellier to marry Parisian taxi driver Odilon Albaret. Since they had no children and she had time on her hands, he volunteered her to run errands for his best client, the writer Marcel

Proust, independently wealthy but confined by chronic asthma to a sprawling apartment at 102 Boulevard Haussmann.

Celeste learned to accommodate her new employer's homosexuality, and well as his unconventional way of life. Proust slept by day. At night, he might have Odilon drive him to dine with friends at the Ritz or to an assignation at one of the two gay *hotels de passe* in which he had a financial interest. Otherwise he stayed in bed and worked on his novel, a masterpiece of retrieved memory which recreated in lapidary detail his childhood and early adulthood. Walls lined with cork muffled the sounds of the city, and his upstairs neighbors justified paying their servants a stingy 50 francs a month with the promise that Proust would give them 100 francs extra if they agreed to wear slippers all day and walk softly around the apartment.

The new young woman's silent efficiency soon made her indispensible. Once war was declared in 1914 and Odilon was called up, Proust fired his former housekeeper and her husband, who had become lazy and overbearing. Céleste replaced them as his sole connection with the outside world, protecting him from distraction and ministering to his declining health. She was still doing so when he died in 1922.

It didn't concern Proust that the uneducated Céleste was ignorant of his world, and of Paris in general. He even had to explain that "Napoléon" and "Bonaparte" were the same person. Her simplicity was comforting; there was more than enough sophistication in his life already. "Nobody on earth knows me better than you do," he told her. "You know all about me. I tell you everything." Asked why they became so close, she explained, "we were both orphans, he with his parents dead and his friends scattered, and I with my parents dead, my family far away, and my husband in the army. So we created our own sort of intimacy, though for him it was chiefly an atmosphere within which to work."

She uncomplainingly adjusted her life to his. He woke when others were going to bed, and wrote through the night. She remained alert to adjust his pillows or bedding, and to bring him his manuscript notebooks. During his hours of sleep she seldom left the apartment, since he sometimes had asthma attacks, which he controlled by igniting a sachet of aromatics, filling his bedroom with pungent smoke.

Such rapport between servant and employer was almost unknown in France at the time. Only a few years earlier, in 1900, Octave Mirbeau had exposed the reality of domestic service in *Diary of a Chambermaid,* the fictionalized memoirs of a young maid, also named Célestine. None of her employers regard her as an intimate. To them, she is barely human. They speak freely in front of her, allowing her to eavesdrop on some outrageous conversations. "One day, I found [Madame] in her boudoir with a friend, describing how, with Monsieur, she'd visited a brothel where they'd watched two little hunchbacks having sex. 'You should see them, my dear,' I overheard Madame say. 'Nothing's more exciting.' "

In contrast to Célestine, Céleste took little interest in sex. When Odilon returned to Paris on a 48-hour leave, she wouldn't go to bed with him until Proust was asleep, and remained alert for his call. She also refused to believe stories of his homoerotic activities, and scoffed at Jean Cocteau's account of Proust's particular fetish, watching young men torturing caged rats with red-hot hatpins. "How dare people print such nonsense!" she wrote. "M. Proust always had a holy terror of rats; so much so, he told me once in passing, that he couldn't even bear the sight of them." Nevertheless he did confide to her that, on a visit to one of these places, he watched a man being whipped. This alarmed her less, since it wasn't Proust who did the whipping, while she could see that he didn't enjoy the experience but thought only of where to fit the episode into the book.

On one occasion, needing to hear once again the César Franck string quartet that inspired a passage in the book, Proust hired musicians to perform it in the apartment, starting at 2 a.m. Céleste stayed awake and prepared fried potatoes as a snack for the players but didn't listen to the music. She saw only its effect on him. "He was transfigured and lit from within," she wrote. "It was with experiences such as this that he managed to keep the flame of life alight within himself. He kept it alight only for his work, which was consuming him." The musicians enjoyed playing in his cork-lined room. "I don't think we've ever sounded so good," said one. "Certainly not at three in the morning," another responded sourly.

Proust trusted Céleste alone with his manuscript. After he drifted into sleep, she gathered the notebooks filled with spidery writing that often spilled over onto separate sheets of paper and pasted his additions onto the edges of the old. By the time he finished, one *cahier* had a chain of attachments more than two meters long.

Céleste's account of Proust's death is touching. As his brother Robert, a doctor, emerged from the bedroom, she demanded, "You are going to save him, aren't you?" "He was very moved," she continued. "He took both my hands and answered, 'Madame, I know all you have done for him. You must be brave. It is all over.' I couldn't stand upright for exhaustion and grief. But I couldn't believe it. He had died so nobly, without a shudder, without a gasp, without the life and the light of the soul vanishing from the eyes looking on us to the end."

Proust had told her "It is your beautiful little hands that will close my eyes." To do so was her last act for the man she had come to love. For decades she refused to speak of her years with him but in the early 1970s, when she was 82, she gave a series of interviews to journalist George Belmont. The resulting book, *Monsieur Proust,* was a best seller, confirming the writer's iconic status in world literature, and celebrating a great, if physically unconsummated, love.

~ ❖ ~

Footnote. Proust left Céleste and Odilon well provided for. They opened a small hotel on the quiet left bank thoroughfare of rue des Canettes. It is currently the 3-star Hôtel la Perle. Neither on the façade or inside is there any reference to Céleste or Proust.

Chapter 7.

THE LOVERS OF MONTPARNASSE: AMEDEO MODIGLIANI AND JEANNE HÉBUTERNE

New to Paris in 1914, English painter and model Nina Hamnett, hailed as the queen of London's bohemia, ate her first French meal at a small restaurant on rue Campagne-Première in Montparnasse. Its Italian owner, Rosalie Robia, herself a former model, extended credit to artists. They repaid her with drawings that she used to decorate her walls.

"I sat down alone and began my dinner," Hamnett wrote. "Suddenly the door opened and in came a man with a roll of newspaper under his arm. He wore a black hat and a corduroy suit. He had curly black hair and brown eyes and was very good looking. He came straight up to me and said, pointing to his chest, *Je suis Modigliani, Juif, Jew,'* unrolled his newspaper and produced some drawings. *'Cinq francs.'* "

Some of the art on display in the restaurant was by this man but, after eight years in Paris, Amedeo Modigliani had sold almost nothing. The elongated, expressionless faces of his portraits and sculptures, inspired by the same African figures that influenced both Picasso and Brancusi, were too cryptic for a market still lulled by impressionism. The stares of those stylized almond-shaped eyes left people unnerved. Even Rosalie expressed doubts about his "squiggles," leading to arguments during which Modigliani indignantly demanded the return of his work. She didn't dare confess that she'd used many of his drawings to light the stove and as toilet paper.

Paris might not know "Modi" as an artist but he had accumulated a reputation as a drinker, singer and *tombeur* or seducer. Like many short, charismatic men (he was only 5 feet, 5 inches tall), he was sexually successful. "How handsome he was, do you know?" recalled Robia. "Holy Virgin! All the women ran after him." In the winter of 1911, he had a brief affair with Russian poet Anna Akhmatova. One of her poems contained a snapshot of their encounter: "In the bluish fog of Paris/And probably Mo-

Amedeo Modigliani

digliani again/Wandering quietly behind me/Sadly . . . " American poet T.S. Eliot, also in Paris at the time, included in his *Humouresque* a stanza that captured something of Modi's contradictory charm. "Half bullying, half imploring air/Mouth twisted to the latest tune;/His who-the-devil-are-you stare. . . "

Unlike most of the art community, Modigliani always bathed, even in the coldest weather. He also paid attention to what he wore, and sneered at friends such as Picasso who dressed like a laborer. His suits, bought second-hand in one of the city's *marchés aux puces,* were generally black but, occasionally, sky blue or yellow. They gave him a dashing air, helped by two items copied from flamboyant singer/ performer Aristide Bruant, a crimson scarf and a wide black hat.

Modigliani believed, like the poets Charles Baudelaire and Arthur Rimbaud, that art depended on a derangement of the senses. His family in Livorno sent a small monthly

Jeanne Hébuterne (1898–1920) in Modigliani's studio on rue de la Grande-Chaumière, in Montparnasse. c. 1918

allowance but he spent that in a few days to induce a creative delirium with absinthe and hashish. Friends hid his money so that enough would remain for food and rent. After his death, Nina Hamnett opened one of the books inherited from him, and a 100 franc note fell out, secreted there and forgotten.

"He had a large studio," recalled Hamnett, "which was very untidy. The bed was unmade. Attached to the end of the bed was an enormous spider-web and in the middle an enormous spider. He explained that he could not make the bed as he had grown very much attached to the spider and was afraid of disturbing it." But he lost the studio for not paying rent and was reduced to sleeping on park benches or the floors of friends, accelerating the progress of his tuberculosis.

Inspired by Impressionism, amateurs from around the world gravitated to Paris in the first days of the new century. The prestigious École des Beaux Arts accepted only a handful into its four-year program, and those after a rigorous exam. (Among those who failed it was Henri Matisse.) It also charged high fees, and excluded women. The private Académie Julian and Académie Carmen were less demanding, but still expensive. Having James McNeill Whistler as a teacher made the latter so popular with young American women that the proprietor, a former model for Whistler, charged them double.

Entrepreneurs exploited the shortage of tuition by opening art schools along Montparnasse's rue de la Grande Chaumière, a few meters from bohemia's preferred hangout, the Café Rotonde. Most professionals scorned the Académie Colarossi and Académie de la Grande Chaumière, one calling them "a ramshackle set of studios where artists and students could pay to use the models and receive a little tutoring if they wished," but they met a demand. Students paid by the class: as little as 50 centimes a session and even less if they bought a book of tickets. There were no entry requirements, and women were welcome. Other innovations included evening sessions under electric light for artists with day jobs.

The atmosphere could be oppressive. "All the rooms were packed," complained one student. "In the one where we were drawing from the nude, the air was stifling because of an overheated stove. We were positively melting in an inferno permeated by the strong smell of perspiring bodies mixed with scent, fresh paint, damp waterproofs and dirty feet; all this was intensified by the thick smoke from cigarettes and the strong tobacco of pipe smokers." Men grabbed the best spots in class, banishing women to the back of the room. No concessions were made to modesty. One innocent arrived just as the teacher was selecting the day's model. After gaping at the succession of nude men who bounded up onto the dais and struck a pose, she fled to the toilet and threw up.

Nobody expected to see an artist as gifted as Modigliani in such surroundings. Yet he was often found there, sketching a model whom he would otherwise have had to hire. When class ended, he walked to the Rotonde and circulated, dashing off portraits for a franc, or even just a shot of absinthe. When, occasionally, he won a commission, he almost perversely muffed it. A baroness proud of her figure commissioned her portrait in a crimson hunting jacket. Modi didn't care for the color of her *redingote*, and painted it as orange. *Madame la baronne*, not surprisingly, declined to pay.

In 1917 a new student appeared at the Colorassi. Jeanne Hébuterne was only 17 but in her large eyes, wide mouth and the red/brown hair that cascaded below her waist Modigliani saw the serene beauty of the women who inspired the masters of the *cinquecento*. Across the English Channel, her near-twin Lizzie Siddall would mesmerize Dante Gabriel Rossetti and the Pre-Raphaelite brotherhood, inspiring some of their most vividly idealized portraits.

Grabbing Russian sculptor Chana Orloff, Modi demanded that she introduce the newcomer. This probably happened at the Rotonde in March 1917 but another story places the meeting at one of the *bals jardins* or outdoor dance parties that took place in private parks on New Year's Eve. Such occasions required a costume, and a legend claims that Jeanne first saw Modi dressed as Pierrot, the sad, mute, white-clad clown of the *commedia dell'arte*.

Léopold Zborowski, Modi's agent, found him a studio at 8 rue de la Grande-Chaumière, next to the Académie Colorossi, and Jeanne, defying her middle-class parents, devoutly Catholic and pathologically anti-Semitic, moved in. He painted her obsessively, emphasizing her placid expression, long neck, auburn hair and the white skin that earned her the childhood nickname *Noix de Coco*

(Coconut). Her eyes were green but in his canvases they were always an ethereal and innocent blue.

That she was the love of his life didn't blind him to the practical advantages of living with someone who could hold a pose for the time necessary to complete a painting, but who cost him nothing. A good model was jealously guarded. When they shared a studio at the Bateau-Lavoir in Montmartre, Pablo Picasso always locked the door on his companion Fernande Olivier if he went out, fearing Modi might lure her away.

When Jeanne became pregnant and German artillery began randomly bombarding Paris, Zborowski sent them to the Riviera. In Nice, on November 29, 1918, Jeanne had a daughter. The birth certificate gave her name as Giovanna but didn't list a father. She became a Modigliani when Modi's sister adopted the baby after his death, and renamed her Jeanne in memory of her mother.

In the fall of 1919, they returned to Paris, where Jeanne once again became pregnant. Zborowski was at last selling Modi's work. A collector in Marseilles bought ten landscapes and scenes in maternity hospitals created during his time in Nice. British writers Osbert and Sacheverell Sitwell also included 59 items in a show of modern French art in London. But the artist treated success with the same contempt as failure. Rather than sell a drawing for less than he thought it worth, he told a dealer to wipe his arse with it, and when a collector asked him to sign a sketch, scrawled his name in huge letters across the image, making it worthless.

He and Jeanne barely survived the winter of 1919-1920. Exacerbated by poor diet, no heating and his usual immoderate consumption of alcohol, Modi's health deteriorated. Tuberculosis invaded his brain, inducing meningitis, which, before antibiotics, was invariably fatal. In January 1920, a neighbor, not having seen the couple for days, found a delirious Modigliani in bed, cradled by Jeanne, who was six months pregnant. He had fallen in the street and laid for hours in the snow before strangers brought him home. Taken to the Hôpital de la Charité, he died on January 24, 1920 at age 36.

Modi was buried in Père Lachaise Cemetery, "like a prince," said one mourner, in a ceremony attended by most of Paris's artistic community. The next morning, at 4 a.m., Jeanne threw herself from the fifth-floor window of her parents' home, killing herself and her unborn child. Her pious family refused to allow the body of a suicide in the house, even that of their own daughter, so friends trundled her corpse on a hand cart to the apartment on rue de la Grand Chaumière, where they sat with it through the night, sharing a bottle and protecting the body from rats.

At Jeanne's funeral, which the family insisted should take place at the Cimetière de Bagneux, a newer cemetery on the outskirts of Paris, as distant as possible from Montparnasse, her parents, in a notable display of bad manners, scorned the tradition of shaking hands with mourners after the interment, keeping their hands pointedly behind their backs. Her body remained at Bagneux for ten years until they relented and allowed it to be exhumed and reburied next to Modi.

~ ❖ ~

Footnote. Jeanne continued to draw, paint and dabble in jewelry design throughout her brief life, but the few surviving examples of her work are mediocre. Nor did other painters for whom she modeled, including Chaim Soutine and Tsuguharu Foujita, see in her the transcendental glow that illuminated Modigliani's canvases. Beauty, as always, was in the eye of the beholder.

Chapter 8.

HELLO, LITTLE SCHOOLGIRL: COLETTE AND WILLY

I n the last decade of the 19th century, the author Henry Gau-
thier-Villars, better known as Willy, frequently visited the Bur-
gundian village of St-Sauveur-en-Puisaye, ostensibly to see his old
comrade-in-arms from the war of 1871, Jules-Joseph Colette. On
his way back to the railway station, however, he detoured to a secluded barn to enjoy his real reason for the visit—sex with his
friend's teenage daughter Sidonie-Gabrielle, 14 years his junior.

Today we'd regard such a relationship as in poor taste, if not illegal, but nobody thought so at the time, least of all Sidonie-Gabrielle. She appreciated a man who though, in her frank description,
"bald, bearded and bulging," offered more satisfaction, both physical and intellectual, than the local clods. May/September unions
were common as women favored husbands sufficiently wealthy to
keep them in comfort while men sought partners young enough
to bear children. Once she became a writer, Colette's stories often

Colette, Willy and the dog, Toby, c. 1905

dealt with such relationships. In *Gigi,* the daughter of a family of courtesans marries an older *ami de famille* whom she has always thought of as a kind of uncle, while the ageing *grande horizontale* of *Cheri* connives with the mother of her boy toy to find him a wife of his own age.

When she was 20, Sidonie-Gabrielle escaped from the boredom of village life by marrying Willy and moving to Paris. As part of the transformation, she discarded her former Christian names, preferring to be known simply as Colette. Having learned that her husband employed a team of writers to ghost his books, she tried writing one herself, starting with stories of her country childhood. Her accounts of nature and wildlife bored Willy, but later, having heard her describe her adolescent lesbian adventures, he decided they had promise. "You ought to jot down on paper some memories of your schooldays," he told her. "Don't be afraid of racy details." When she skimped on these, he locked her in her bedroom until she produced *Claudine à l'Ecole—Claudine At School*. Two more novels followed, describing Claudine's move to Paris, then her marriage, and finally her emergence as an independent woman. All were best sellers.

The Claudine books resonated with the androgynous *garçonne* style then popular in bohemian circles. Noting that lesbians had taken to wearing a mannish white collar and tie *à la* Claudine, often adding a monocle and a white carnation in the buttonhole, Willy, seeing his protégée outgrowing him, rushed to keep ahead of her, promoting the Claudine mystique, licensing Claudine soap, Claudine perfume, a Claudine doll, and adapting the books for the theater.

Willy's friends expected Colette to be scandalized by his philandering but she viewed it with amusement, and herself took lovers of both sexes, at one point even sharing one of his partners, the wealthy bisexual American Georgie Raoul-Duval. *Claudine à Paris* incorporated such a liaison, to the horror of Raoul-Duval, who bought up the entire printing and had them burned. Willy simply sold the book to another publisher and pocketed two advances.

In 1902, a stage version of *Claudine à Paris* featured Émilie Marie Bouchaud, a wasp-waisted young actress with a mass of tight black curls who took the name Polaire. "The agitating and agitated Polaire!" rhapsodized a critic. "Her great voracious mouth, the immense black eyes, ringed, bruised, discolored, the incandescence of her pupils, the bewildered nocturnal hair, the phosphorus, the sulphur, the red pepper of that ghoulish, Salome-like face!"

Willy encouraged the public perception that Polaire and Colette were lovers, and that he sometimes shared their bed. He dressed them identically, and appeared in public with one on each arm. He was photographed for postcards playing Polaire's "protector," lacing up her corset, scolding her, and admiring her in male trousers. Jean Cocteau drew the girls chatting at a café table, watched askance by the owner but with proprietorial satisfaction by Willy.

To nobody's surprise, the marriage barely survived into the new century. Colette, having outgrown Willy, divorced him in 1906 and, swearing off Paris, novels and men, moved into the chateau of a new friend, Mathilde, Marquise de Morny. At a time when women needed a police permit to wear male clothing in public, "Missy" de Morny exploited her wealth and position to dress as a man, smoke cigars and carry on flagrant lesbian affairs. When the couple bought a holiday house at Saint-Coulomb in Brittany, its owner, Baron du Crest, refused to close the deal at the last minute when the marquise arrived in male clothing, so Colette signed the deed instead.

Ambitious to appear on stage, Colette, with de Morny, conceived *Rêve d'Égypte—Dream of Egypt*, a mime drama in which the marquise, playing a male Egyptologist, unearths the tomb of a princess—Colette. After the Prefect of Police tried to have it banned, no theater would stage it, so she and de Morny took it to Montmartre's most notorious cabaret, the Moulin Rouge, where the show debuted in January 1907.

"The Moulin Rouge was packed," wrote a reporter. "It was also ultra elegant; tailcoats and evening gowns filled the private boxes." De Morny's first appearance caused an uproar. "From the moment when, under the brown suit, we recognize the marquise," a reviewer wrote breathlessly, "the whistles start from all corners, the cries resound, the howls never stop. The uproar redoubles when Colette Willy, coming to life in her sarcophagus, begins to mime a love scene." Under her skimpy costume, Colette appeared to be naked (she actually wore a flesh-colored leotard). The spectators went wild as the scene climaxed in a passionate kiss. "Insults are uttered that we cannot quote," the report continued. "From two upper balconies ladies throw various projectiles, even cushions, onto the stage; the whole room, standing up, boos the two performers in a final outburst of disapproval."

Someone recognized Willy among the spectators. "He wants to leave his box," wrote the reporter, "but he is surrounded, escorted, jostled and sometimes beaten by two or three hundred people who hustle him out of the room, shouting. The ushers strive to protect the exit of the unfortunate, while fights break out between demonstrators, requiring the intervention of the Republican Guard and the police."

As a declaration of social and sexual independence, *Rêve d'Égypte* was a spectacular success, shocking even Willy. Although they had been technically divorced for four years, it motivated him to finalize the decree. The naive country girl had outstripped the master.

Colette would continue to live as an independent woman, finding intellectual and sexual satisfaction on her own terms. In 1924, at age 52, she had an affair with her 16-year-old stepson, Bertrand de Jouvenel. A year later, Maurice Goudeket, 16 years her junior, became her third husband. These relationships inspired one of her finest stories, *Le Blé en Herbe—Ripening Seed,* in which a boy who has spent summers at the same seaside resort from infancy is seduced by an older woman. The experience alerts him to the attractions of a girl his own age whom he has never thought of except as a playmate.

Until her death in 1954, Colette never lost the appetite for life that sustained her through a tumultuous career. Her vivacity survived even being confined to a wheelchair. Retiring to an apartment in the Palais Royale, in the heart of fashionable Paris, she would have herself carried down to the elegant Grand Vefour restaurant to share lunch with her neighbour Jean Cocteau. "Whenever I despair," she wrote, "I no longer expect my end, but some bit of luck, some commonplace little miracle which, like a glittering link, will mend again the necklace of my days."

~ ❖ ~

Footnote. In later years, when he fell on hard times, Willy, without Colette's knowledge, sold the rights to the Claudine books. At the same time, he ordered an assistant to burn the original manuscripts, which showed she had written them. Fortunately his order was disobeyed, and Colette was able to prove authorship and retrieve the rights.

Chapter 9.

LOVE FOR SALE: GLORIA SWANSON AND HENRY DE LA FALAISE, MARQUIS DE LA COUDRAYE

At the turn of 19th century, a booming American economy created scores of new millionaires who, denied social acceptance by their own aristocracy, hoped to raise their status overseas. In 1894, Anna Gould, daughter of multimillionaire Jay Gould and possessor of a personal fortune, in today's money, of half a billion US dollars, married Marie Ernest Paul Boniface, Comte de Castellane-Novejean, Marquis de Castellane, otherwise known as Boni de Castellane, one of the handsomest men in France, but also among the most impoverished. The new marquise was short, chubby, of sullen disposition, with a premature "dowager's hump" and a permanent frown, but as de Castellane put it, "she is not deficient in the matter of her dowry."

After that, it was open season on anyone listed in Europe's index to titled families, the *Almanach de Gotha*. So blatant was the annual voyage to Europe by predatory heiresses that they became known as "the Fishing Fleet." Movie star Pola Negri married Georgian aristocrat Serge Mdivani and Mae Murray his brother David, after which every actress wanted her name in the social register. Gloria Swanson, America's most successful star, refused to apologize for this unseemly traffic. "The public wanted us to live like kings and queens, so we did—and why not? We were in love with life. We were making more money than we ever dreamed existed and there was no reason to believe it would ever stop."

Swanson, already twice divorced, arrived in Paris in 1925 to appear in *Madame Sans-Gêne (Madame Without Manners)*. The most lavish film of her career, it used the palace of Versailles and other authentic locations to tell the story of the laundress who befriended Napoléon as a junior officer, married one of his marshals, and scandalized society with her outspoken and uninhibited behavior.

Publicist for the production was handsome young André Daven. He had just ended an association—and, some claimed, a love affair—with Rudolph Valentino, who brought him to Hollywood and tried, unsuccessfully, to launch him as an actor. An accomplished intriguer, Daven suggested his friend Charles Boyer for the role of Napoléon in *Madame Sans-Gêne*. Boyer auditioned, but the tiny 5' 1" Swanson decided he was too tall.

Asked to hire a translator, Daven recruited another friend, the Marquis Henri de la Falaise de Coudraye. Attached to the American Expeditionary Forces during World War I while still in his teens, Coudraye won the Croix de Guerre and sustained a number of wounds. "He was a real war hero," said another actress, Lillian Gish, admiringly. "In his bathing suit he presents a graphic picture of what modern warfare does to a man, he is so cut and shot and covered with scars."

Swanson and the dashing Coudraye immediately became lovers. When she got pregnant, her first impulse was to keep the child, since she had already been tricked into an abortion by the first of her eventual five husbands, the actor Wallace Beery. However, her studio, Famous Players-Lasky, advised against it. Not only would a child impair her vamp image; she was still technically married to her third husband, which would complicate the question of paternity. Daven arranged the termination. He was also a witness at the discreet wedding in January 1925 before the couple returned to America, to be greeted by parades in New York and Los Angeles.

The studio pulled out all the stops for the New York premiere of *Madame Sans-Gêne,* as The *New York Times* reported.

Gloria Swanson with her husband,
Henry de la Falaise, 1925

"Long before the hour fixed for the opening of the film, the streets in the neighborhood were all but blocked by a crowd of literally thousands of the curious eager to catch a fleeting glimpse of the new Marquise de la Coudray and her French husband. The throng was so dense that many of the guests of the producers had to fight their way from their automobiles to the doors of the theatre. Policemen were kept busy escorting dazzling women and their escorts into the theater and after the show there was a terrific crush on the carpeted pavement. Outside, the theater was decorated with tricolor streamers, and Napoleonic soldiers stood stolidly on guard just outside two sentry boxes. Half the audience spent a large share of its time in staring at the balcony wherein sat the evening's star of filmdom. The film itself was a secondary affair. . . ."

Behind the scenes, Coudraye's role of trophy husband soon began to chafe. When skeptical pressmen questioned the authenticity of his title, he defended himself with vigor. "My family name is Le Bailly," he said, "but I could add at least 24 other titles of small estates under which I might live. My entire name is really James Henry Le Bailly de la Falaise, Marquis de la Coudraye. But in the United States I am generally called Hank." He tried to start his own company to make documentary films on remote locations, but Swanson, who suffered a prolonged depression following her abortion and preferred to keep him close to home, bullied him into a desk job with the French Pathé company.

Breaking with Famous Players-Lasky, Swanson became her own producer, with catastrophic results. Joseph P. Kennedy, father of the future president, bailed her out. At his urging, she fired most of her staff and sold the rights to her early films, investing the profits in the massive and financially disastrous production of *Queen Kelly*, directed by Erich von Stroheim. She and Kennedy also became lovers, so Coudraye began an affair with actress Constance Bennett, whom he married when he and Swanson divorced in 1930. Swanson went on to two more marriages, neither of them happy. She and Coudraye remained friends, however. Many years later, reviewing her life, she wrote, "My marriage to Henri gave me the only real peace and happiness I had ever known—or have ever known since. Of my five marriages this one came the nearest to being what I, in my *hausfrau* heart, have always wanted a marriage to be. He was then and he remains in memory a more delightful companion than any I have known."

~❖~

Footnote: Swanson returned to the spotlight in Billy Wilder's 1950 drama *Sunset Boulevard.* As forgotten silent star Norma Desmond, she spends evenings running her films, for which Wilder used clips from *Queen Kelly.* Operating the projector is her butler and major-domo, played by *Queen Kelly*'s director, von Stroheim.

Chapter 10.

JULES AND JIM AND OTHERS: HENRI-PIERRE ROCHÉ AND FRANZ AND HELEN HESSEL

Not all great loves blossom in the glare of publicity. Some germinate in darkness and mature in secret, seeing the light only when the principals choose to go public. One relationship destined to become famous in French literary history took place between the world wars but wasn't revealed until 1953, when Henri-Pierre Roché published his novel *Jules et Jim*.

Dignified, rail-thin, over six feet tall, always impeccably dressed and with a pipe clamped in his teeth, Roché was a familiar figure in the art world. Even as a young man he knew every important painter in Paris, including Pablo Picasso, to whom he introduced Gertrude Stein and her brother Leo, the earliest collectors of his work. Leo Stein remembered Roché as "a tall man with an inquiring eye under an inquisitive forehead, [who] wanted to

LES FILMS DU CARROSSE et S.E.D.I.F.

JEANNE MOREAU

DANS

UN FILM DE
FRANÇOIS TRUFFAUT

**JULES
et
JIM**

D'APRÈS LE ROMAN DE
HENRI-PIERRE ROCHÉ
ADAPTATION ET DIALOGUE DE
FRANÇOIS TRUFFAUT et JEAN GRUAULT

**OSKAR WERNER
HENRI SERRE**

MARIE DUBOIS

ET DE LA PHOTOGRAPHIE
RAOUL COUTARD

MUSIQUE DE
GEORGES DELERUE

Jules et Jim poster, 1962

know something more about everything. He knew everybody and wanted everybody to know everybody else."

If any book was expected from Roché, it would have been the memoir of a career spent in the company of artists and the appreciation and acquisition of art. Instead, *Jules et Jim*, published towards the end of his life, fictionalized a key episode in a life largely devoted to sexual experiment.

It describes how, at the turn of the century, Jim, a Parisian intellectual, befriends Jules, a young German writer. Jules wants to attend the infamous Quatz'arts costume ball, where artists and models dress—and undress—to exhibit their lack of inhibition. Jim invites him as his guest and they visit a costumier together to chose outfits, the beginning of a life-long friendship.

In time, both fall in love with the free-spirited Kate, but she marries Jules. When the three meet again after World War I, however, Kate confides her unhappiness to Jim who, with the approval of Jules, moves in with them. Their *ménage à trois*, however, isn't as harmonious as they hoped. Kate proves more sexually adventurous than either, making love to both but also inviting another man into her bed. "In her mind," Roché writes, "each lover was a separate world, and what happened in one world was no concern of the others. But this didn't prevent her from being jealous herself." Unable to reconcile these conflicts, she drives their car into a river with Jim as a passenger. Paradoxically, he is elated to have been chosen to join her in death. "She turned to him with a mischievous, comradely glance, as if they had plenty of time; as if they were once more setting out on a journey of adventure together. Her glance said: 'You see, Jim, I've won this time.' The archaic smile had never been so pure . . . . He let himself be drawn passively into her splendor."

The story behind *Jules et Jim* became more widely known when François Truffaut filmed it. *Jules et Jim* (1962), starring Oskar Werner, Henri Serre and Jeanne Moreau, enjoyed enormous success, despite efforts to suppress it by the French authorities, who branded as "immoral" its skeptical view of conventional marriage. When the film made the book a belated bestseller, people discovered that it was based on fact, and wanted to know more about the real characters. What they found was unexpected.

From adolescence, Serre, Henri-Pierre Roché's interest in art was matched by a curiosity about sex. He began by seducing housemaids and, as a student, graduated to the *vendeuses* and *midinettes* of Montmartre. In diaries and letters he documented his liaisons in forensic detail, comparing and contrasting his partners and their attributes. As his attraction to a woman faded, he passed her on to friends, often sharing her with them during the transition. Alarmed at his preoccupation with sex, his mother sent him to a clinic that practiced hydrotherapy, plunging patients repeatedly into baths of icy water. It had no effect.

Roché planned a career in the foreign service, but one of his college tutors, fearing international incidents if he were let loose in the corridors of diplomacy, urged that he widen his horizons. "The French have shut themselves away behind their frontiers far too long," he said. "They should travel. You will always find some newspaper to pay for your escapades."

Roché hesitated to do so alone until the 1906 Quatz'arts Ball. Watching two women putting on a spontaneous demonstration of lesbian lovemaking, he noticed another young man also taking an interest. Austrian Franz Hessel was as passive as Roché was adventurous. Once they became friends, Roché described his plan for a kind of erotic Grand Tour, inspired by his tutor's suggestion, and invited Hessel to join him—which, as the son of a successful Jewish banker, he could afford to do.

They traveled through Europe for months, visiting brothels, and seducing and exchanging partners, Roché always setting the pace, Hessel amiably joining in or looking on. On a Greek island, both were transfixed by the sculpture of a woman with an enigmatic smile. *Jules et Jim* describes how they "lingered round the goddess in silence, gazing at her from different angles. Her smile was a floating presence, powerful, youthful, thirsty for kisses and perhaps for blood."

When they passed through Germany, Franz introduced Roché to Helen Grund, who, over the objections of her gentile military family, he intended to marry. Jeanne Moreau's portrayal in the film became the accepted version of Helen but her brunette vivacity and humor didn't resemble the real Helen, who was slight, blue-eyed and blonde, with long hair that fell almost to her waist. She displayed an imperious quality that Roché found both provocative and challenging. He immediately understood her appeal, and her threat: she shared the Greek statue's inscrutable smile.

Hessel married Grund, but though the marriage produced two sons, neither Franz nor Helen were happy, the two often living apart and, in her case, pursuing other relationships. When Roché met them again in 1920, his presence appeared to fill a gap in the lives of both, and for three weeks, in the village outside Munich where the Hessels were holidaying, they shared a three-way sexual idyll, joined, from time to time, by another of Helen's lovers.

Indifferent to the disapproval of the locals, the men sunbathed nude in the garden, and Helen strolled through the village dressed as a man, complete with false moustache. Such walks began playfully, but could turn violent. One evening, she spontaneously threw herself into the river, trusting the men to rescue her. She also carried a vial of acid in her purse, "for the eyes of men who tell lies," she informed them ominously. Her escapades alerted Roché to an imbalance in Helen's character, which partly explained the failed marriage.

Roché's pursuit of sexual pleasure continued between the wars. Soon after Man Ray arrived in Paris in 1921, Roché visited his studio to be photographed for a portrait. Ray showed him "some very moving pictures of lesbians, in eight most luscious poses. I knew one of these beautiful girls. Then, two photos of love-making between a man and a woman." The "beautiful girls" were Surrealist artist Méret Oppenheim and Maria "Nusch" Benz, who succeeded Gala as the wife of poet Paul Éluard, while the couple having sex were probably Ray and his mistress and model Alice Prin, alias Kiki de Montparnasse. Roché bought the photographs and commissioned more of the same.

The Hessels divorced in 1921 and Helen moved to Paris to live with Roché, only to return to Germany the following year and remarry Franz, then take her sons to Paris once again in 1925 and live with Roché until 1928. She hoped she might have children with Roché but by 1934 realized he had no such intention, and broke off their relationship. He did marry and have a son, but not until later in life. "I'm sleeping with three women," he joked cynically, "so I'll marry the one who lives longest." His son remembered him as remote, frequently absent, grudging in his affection, and the marriage as turbulent, racked with domestic arguments.

When the Hessel family lost their money in the 1929 crash, Franz became a book editor and translator, working with Walter Benjamin on the German edition of Proust's *À la Recherche du Temps Perdu,* while Helen returned to Paris as fashion correspondent for the *Frankfurter Zeitung.* Roché continued his busy sex life, which he documented systematically. His family's real estate holdings included a building used as a brothel, in which he took an active interest. He also rented an apartment to which he invited women chosen at random, often from personal advertisements in the newspapers. After seducing them, he recorded their sexual tastes and fantasies, an early step on the path followed later by Kinsey and Masters and Johnson.

He also belatedly joined the French diplomatic service, which allowed him to research women on both sides of the Atlantic. While living in New York, he seduced young Dadaist Beatrice Wood, and through her met *avant garde* artist Marcel Duchamp. They became friends, and carried on a long correspondence. Wood, resigned to being a "monogamous woman in a polygamous world," slept with both.

Throughout the German occupation of France, Helen lived in Paris with her sons, the younger of whom, Stephane, became active in the resistance and was arrested, but survived Buchenwald. Franz, as a Jew, was imprisoned in Germany but released due to poor health and deported to France after the intercession of Helen and the wife of painter Francis Picabia. He died there in 1941.

Of the trio, Helen was the strongest. "Whatever suited her was important," said one of her sons. "She didn't care too much whether other people went along. Also, she didn't necessarily treat very well the men who were in love with her." The mercurial nature of their tripartite affair was captured in the lyrics to *Le Tourbillion (The Whirlwind)*, Cyrus Bassiak's theme song for Truffaut's film. "We knew each other, we recognized each other/ We lost sight of each other, we lost sight of each other again/We found each other, then we separated. Every man for himself/In the whirlwind of life"

~ ❖ ~

Footnote. Helen Hessel attended the premiere of the film, but declined to be interviewed by the press. Jeanne Moreau suggested that the relationship between Roché and the Hessels was not so much a *ménage à trois* as two conjoined love affairs, one of them between the two men, to which the presence of Helen provided a catalyst. Beatrice Wood went on to become an important figure in the Dada movement, lived to 105, and inspired the centenarian *Titanic* survivor played by Gloria Stuart in James Cameron's 1997 film.

Chapter 11.

MAD ABOUT THE BOY: JEAN COCTEAU AND RAYMOND RADIGUET

I t took years for France to recover from the trauma of World War I. The *annus mirabilis,* at least for Paris and the arts, would be 1922, bringing James Joyce's *Ulysses,* the last volume of *À La Recherche du Temps Perdu* (as well as the death of its author), and the birth of the most innovative of Paris cabarets, *Le Boeuf sur le Toit.* Flashing across the sky in 1919 and 1920 like a harbinger of these events was Raymond Radiguet.

His mop of black hair, aquiline nose, sensitive mouth, augmented by what Nina Hamnett called "white, regular teeth and greenish-grey eyes," made Raymond stand out among the seven children of magazine illustrator and cartoonist Maurice Radiguet, but even more striking was his intelligence. By the time he dropped out of school at 11 he was intimate with the work of Stendhal, Proust, Verlaine, Mallarmé and Rimbaud. His parents volunteered him to tutor a neighbor, a young teacher whose fiancé was in the army. Alice Saunier, 23, seduced the 14-year-old instead, and for a year they enjoyed an affair under his parents' noses before Raymond, weary of mere sensation, broke it off and migrated to Montparnasse in search of better conversation.

He was soon writing pieces for the satirical magazines, and became a regular in the cafés, particularly the Rotonde, where he socialized with Juan Gris, Pablo Picasso and other members of the Hispanic community. Amedeo Modigliani introduced him to absinthe. Containing 75 percent alcohol and noted for its hallucinogenic qualities, this infusion of wormwood and licorice was outlawed by the French government in 1915 because young men who drank it lost all interest in fighting the Germans. Radiguet practically subsisted on it.

He also hung out with composers Georges Auric, Francis Poulenc and Arthur Honegger of the innovative group *Le Six*. This led him into the orbit of Jean Cocteau, at whose apartment he turned up one day in June 1919. "There's a child at the door, sir," a puzzled servant announced. "A child with a cane!" The flamboyant Cocteau, a prolific painter, writer, playwright and filmmaker, was still mourning his aviator lover Eugène Adrien Roland George Garros, who died in combat during the last days of the war. But Radiguet's looks and intelligence dazzled him. Being twice his age was not an issue. To Cocteau, "a generation is not made up of people of the same age but of people who share the same way of life."

Whether they were sexual partners is uncertain. Cocteau probably considered him more surrogate son than lover. He had a series of such protégés throughout his life, the last of whom, the actor Edouard Dermit, became his legally adopted heir. Every aspect of Radiguet charmed Cocteau, even his faults. "He never cut his hair," he said. "And he was short-sighted but didn't know it. So we bought glasses, which he thought looked awful. Instead, he wore a monocle, which gave him a sneer. This pissed people off, but he said that was what he liked."

Cocteau encouraged Radiguet to write rather than talk away his talent, but this was a struggle, particularly when absinthe was around. "Radiguet could be as wise as an old Chinese sage," he said, "and as mischievous as a schoolboy who climbs out the window to avoid finishing his homework. It's very complicated to explain details to someone who is really a vast glittering factory that runs on alcohol. A *lot* of

Raymond Radiguet, by Man Ray, 1922

alcohol." He could hardly disapprove, however, given his own addiction to opium.

To remove him from temptation, Cocteau spirited Radiguet away to Piquey, a village on the Atlantic coast, where, through the winter of 1921, the young writer, often half-drunk, turned his affair with Alice Saunier into the novel *Le Diable au Corps (Devil in the Flesh)*. Friends came from Paris to enjoy the sight of the usually sarcastic and hypercritical Cocteau posing with Radiguet on the beach and indulging his taste for fancy dress.

Le Diable au Corps was a triumph. Radiguet's insight into sex and passion showed sophistication surprising in a man of any age. "Marthe was mine; and it wasn't I who said so, but she. I could touch her face, kiss her eyes, her arms, dress her, hurt her; she was mine, In my ecstasy I bit her in places where her skin was exposed, so that her mother would suspect that she had a lover. I would have liked to mark her with my initials. In my childish savagery I rediscovered the ancient significance of tattoos. Marthe said 'Yes, bite me, mark me, I want everyone to know.'" Publishers Grasset bought the book immediately. Seeing the promotional possibilities of Radiguet's youth, they filmed him signing the contract as "France's youngest-ever novelist," and arranged for the clip to be screened as part of the most popular weekly newsreel. Nor did they even try to answer the protests that followed publication, some from family groups that disapproved of the sex, but most from veterans who deplored a novel in which a wife cuckolded a soldier even as he huddled in the trenches of the Somme. They were particularly incensed by a scene where, as the couple make love in front of an open fire, she consigns the husband's latest letter to the flames. Radiguet shrugged off their criticism, referring them to the book's opening passage. "Let those who are angry with me keep their memories of the war and leave me and my comrades to have ours. You can't imagine what the war was like for so many very young boys: four years of summer vacation."

Success fuelled Radiguet's arrogance. At the opening of the new jazz cabaret *Le Boeuf sur le Toit,* a pet project of Cocteau, he became bored with the conversation and joined hard-drinking sculptor Konstantin Brancusi at the bar. Late in the evening, the two left, very drunk, in search of a restaurant that served the Provençal fish stew *bouillabaisse.* The one they found was disappointing, so they impulsively boarded a train to Marseilles, hoping the Mediterranean port city and traditional home of the dish would produce a more authentic example. Still unsatisfied, they took a boat to Corsica, where they remained for ten days, drunk on the raw local brandy. Though the trip was never more than a prank, a furious and jealous Cocteau barred Brancusi from the cabaret and never again mentioned him in any of his writing about art.

In the wake of *Le Diable au Corps*, Radiguet was lionized, until Cocteau, seeing him once more being distracted, dragged him away from Paris again, this time to Le Lavandou, a fishing village on the Cote d'Azur. There he started another novel, set in Paris's party-giving Eurotrash aristocracy but based on the 17th century *La Princess de Clèves.*

The reaction to *Le Bal du comte d'Orgel* was enthusiastic but Radiguet didn't live to enjoy it. Rashly, he swam in the notoriously polluted waters of the Seine, and came down a few days later with an infection that physicians initially failed to diagnose as typhoid. By the time they realized their error he was near death. Cocteau was at his bedside to hear his rambling last words. "'Listen,' he said, 'listen to a terrible thing. In three days I will be shot by the soldiers of God.' Choking with tears, I told him that wasn't so. 'Your information,' he continued, 'is not as good as mine. The order is given. I heard the order.' Later he said, 'There is a color that walks around and people hide in this color.' I asked him if they should be chased away. He replied, 'You can't drive them away, since you can't see the color.' He moved his mouth, he spoke our names, he looked with surprise at his mother, at his father, at his hands. Raymond Radiguet begins."

Coco Chanel designed his funeral, which Cocteau was too upset to attend. Watched by a packed congregation of artistic celebrities, with the African-American jazz band from *Le Boeuf sur Le Toit* in the front pews, his body in a white coffin with a bunch of red roses on top was placed in a hearse drawn by four white horses which carried it to Père Lachaise cemetery, the cortege of mourners following on foot in the rain.

Cocteau was right to see the death of Radiguet as a beginning rather than an end. In the century since his death, his reputation and that of his two novels has only increased, helped by a number of film adaptations. The jazz age would soon make it the fashionable ambition to "live fast, die young and have a beautiful corpse" but in this, as in much else, Raymond Radiguet was there first.

~ ❖ ~

Footnote. Radiguet challenged the accepted wisdom about writing and age. "It's a cliché," he wrote, "to say that, to write, one must have lived. But what I would like to know is—why should there be a lower age limit for the right to say, 'I've lived?' It shows, if you think about it, a lot of contempt for young people."

Chapter 12.

THE LEFT BANK: JEAN RHYS, STELLA BOWEN AND FORD MADOX FORD

Britain's traditional prejudice against France discouraged British writers from relocating in the same numbers as Americans, and the few who did do so often brought with them a class consciousness and stifling morality offensive to the *laissez-faire* French. Many claimed to be there for cultural reasons but novelist Michel Georges-Michel wrote mockingly that, "what appealed to them was this moral liberty which they knew neither in London nor in any city of free and austere America; this international *kermesse* of la Rotonde, du Dôme, le Parnasse, where, indiscriminately and at any hour, even on Sunday, they could work, drink, play the piano and dance even with girls whom they did not know and who came gladly to make their acquaintance."

With his bushy moustache, pompous manner and portly build, Ford Madox Hueffer, who changed his name to Ford during World War I because "Hueffer" sounded too Germanic, was almost a parody of the British gentleman, forever pontificating about "the French" and complaining about the "straight, hateful, stony streets" of "Haussmanised" Paris: traits his supporters tried to ignore because of his gifts as a writer. *The Good Soldier* and the four novels of his *Parade's End* series were among the finest to come out of the war, the more so for Ford having fought in the trenches, surviving poison gas attacks and a breakdown induced by "shell shock."

As editor/publisher of *Transatlantic Review,* he championed such writers as Ernest Hemingway, Gertrude Stein and Ezra Pound, but received little thanks in return. Hemingway mocked him in *The Sun Also Rises* as Henry Braddocks, an English writer with a naive wife. Ford found this particularly hurtful. "I helped Joseph Conrad," he complained to his friend Gilbert Seldes. "I helped Hemingway. I helped a dozen, a score of writers, and many of them have beaten me. I'm now an old man and I'll die without making a name like Hemingway."

"At this climax," Seldes continued, "Ford began to sob. Then he began to cry."

In 1924, Ford was living in Paris with Australian painter Stella Bowen, 20 years his junior, when a fragile, lost-looking young woman drifted into Montparnasse. Ella Williams was born on the Caribbean island of Dominica but lived most of her life in England. She moved to Paris, where she married an inept con man named Jean Lenglet. When she met Ford, Lenglet had just been sentenced to a year's imprisonment for fraud, leaving her homeless and broke. With few marketable talents, she pinned her hopes on finding work as a nanny, dancer or artist's model.

Williams had also written a few short stories, and her style, bleak, clipped, and cynical, impressed Ford. He'd been commissioned to translate the novel *Perversité* by Francis Carco but gave the job to her, letting her keep the money but retaining credit for the translation. Once she accumulated enough short fiction, he helped her publish her first collection, *The Left Bank and Other Stories,* and contributed an introduction. "Coming from the West Indies," he wrote, "with a terrifying insight and passion for stating the case of the underdog, she has let her pen loose on the Left Banks of the Old World." Stella Bowen echoed his praise. "She took the lid off the world that she knew, and showed us an underworld of darkness and disorder, where officialdom, the bourgeoisie and the police were the eternal enemies and the fugitive her only hero."

Jean Rhys, Ford Madox Ford, and Stella Bowen

Ford suggested she discard her unglamorous name in favor of the pithier Jean Rhys. He also offered her a bedroom in the house he shared with Bowen. In the case of Ford's earlier houseguests, free board and lodging presupposed their seduction, and the gossips of Montparnasse assumed Rhys would be no different. Bowen was under no illusions about Ford's intentions, and even encouraged them, rationalizing such affairs as essential to his mental wellbeing. "In order to keep his machinery running," she wrote, "he requires to exercise his sentimental talents from time to time upon a new object. It keeps him young. It refreshes his ego. It restores his belief in his power. And who shall say that this type of lubrication is too expensive for so fine a machine?"

Initially, Rhys visited Lenglet every week in the prison at Fresnes, but bowed to Ford's disapproval and stopped doing so. Her life, like Bowen's, came to revolve around him. Bowen gave hints on pleasing him, down to suggesting the kind of clothes he liked, and lending items from her own wardrobe. Of the effect of this on Rhys and the other women he seduced, she was dismissive. As she put it, most women were ready to sacrifice themselves, once they found the right man.

Rhys's first novel, *Quartet,* documented her involvement with the couple. She compared herself and Bowen to "two members of a harem who didn't get on." She also discovered that, for all Ford's philandering, he didn't really like women. "His hands were inexpert, clumsy at caresses, his mouth was hard as he kissed." As the *ménage à trois* continued, Rhys became "brooding, nervous, waiting and hoping for the violent reaction that might free her from an impossible situation." This came with her husband's release in June 1925. Ford and Bowen recoiled from the unshaven, pale, thin and bedraggled Lenglet, and were embarrassed by his stories of prison life. As he was about to be deported to his native Holland, Rhys insisted on sharing his last night in France. When she returned the next day, a furious Ford announced that he had found her a job on the Riviera as a companion to a wealthy American. Rhys accepted immediately and left for Nice. They never met again.

Ford and Bowen separated in 1927, and Ford died in 1939, an increasingly marginal figure. Rhys returned to Britain where her cynicism and bitterness only increased, exacerbated by bouts with alcohol. She married twice, both times to weaker men whom she bullied, in some cases physically attacking them. Episodes of public drunkenness led to convictions for assault and disturbing the peace, and brief spells in prison.

Long after most people assumed she was dead, Rhys emerged from the shadows with the 1966 *Wide Sargasso Sea,* a "prequel" to

Charlotte Brontë's *Jane Eyre* which drew on her Dominican background to tell the story of that book's unseen character, Antoinette Cosway, the Creole heiress who marries Edward Rochester, loses her mind and is kept under guard in an upper room of the house where Jane is employed as a governess. Its depiction of imprisonment and sense of male tyranny was inspired by Rhys's experience with Ford.

Wide Sargasso Sea moved the *New York Times* to call Rhys "the greatest living British novelist." Time had transmuted her despair and misanthropy into a fashionable *ennui,* while her reassessment of Antoinette Cosway as a victim of male dominance played perfectly into contemporary feminism. Even her fragmentary style appealed to the modern ear. "She knows every detail of the shabby world she creates," critic A. Alvarez wrote, "knows precisely how much to leave out—surprisingly much—and precisely how to modulate the utterly personal speaking voice which controls it all, at once casual and poignant, the voice of the loser who refuses, though neither she nor God knows why, to go down."

~ ❖ ~

Footnote. Rhys first wrote *Wide Sargasso Sea* in 1939 but burned the only typescript during a drunken argument. Later she reconstructed it in her head, but didn't commit it to paper again until the 1960s.

Chapter 13.

KICKING THE GONG AROUND: HARRY AND CARESSE CROSBY

F ew expatriates contributed so generously to Paris's reputation for wild living as Harry and Caresse Crosby. Beautiful, arrogant and rich, they could have been among those couples in Scott Fitzgerald's novel *The Great Gatsby,* who, "got into automobiles which bore them out to Long Island and somehow ended up at Gatsby's door. Once there they were introduced by somebody who knew Gatsby and after that they conducted themselves according to the rules of behavior associated with amusement parks."

Crosby would have felt quite at home *chez* Gatsby; the dance floor of the house where he grew up could accommodate 150 people. The nephew of financier J. Pierpont Morgan, he was not so much born with a silver spoon in his mouth as owner of the entire tea service, and gold plated at that. Tall, handsome, intelligent, articulate, brave, he seemed to embody the American ideal, and to be destined for great things.

Opium den in Paris, c. 1928

True to this paradigm, he volunteered in the First World War on the French side while the United States dithered about becoming involved. With Ernest Hemingway, Dashiell Hammett, Walt Disney, Sylvia Beach, e.e. cummings and hundreds of other idealistic or thrill-seeking young Americans, he sailed for France in 1917—only to be rebuffed by the French, who wanted no well-meaning amateurs bumbling around crowded trenches with loaded rifles.

Most, including Hemingway and Crosby, found work with the ambulance and support services. It was while Hemingway was acting as an auxiliary on the Italian front, distributing chocolate and cigarettes, that a mortar round peppered one of his legs with shrapnel. Crosby drove an ambulance during the battle of Verdun, on the Western front, ferrying the wounded to hospital for three days without relief. In a delirium fuelled by exhaustion he saw "the red sun setting back of the hills and the charred skeletons of trees and the river Meuse and the black shells spouting up in columns along the road to Bras and the thunder of the barrage and the wounded and the ride through red explosions and the violent metamorphose from boy to man." His heroism earned the Croix de Guerre.

When a near-direct hit from an artillery shell destroyed his ambulance, wounding others but leaving him untouched, Crosby took it as an indication that Fate had preserved him to experience everything life could offer. Acting on this premise, he returned to Boston and invited his mistress, Polly Peabody, to join him in Paris and, in the slang of the time, "kick the gong around," referring to the gong one struck at opium dens, signaling the attendant to bring a pipe.

Polly was the exact opposite of those women Harry called "Boston virgins who are brought up among sexless surroundings, who wear canvas drawers and flat-heeled shoes." Recently divorced from an alcoholic husband, she had already scandalized Boston's stuffy society by designing and patenting a backless brassiere, and appearing for her wedding with bobbed hair and pink fingernails, wearing a red coat trimmed with monkey fur.

In Paris, the Crosbys, now married, wasted no time in announcing their arrival. They took a house on the Île Saint-Louis, in the middle of the Seine, acquired a grass-green Voisin automobile with a Black chauffeur, and a yacht, which they christened Aphrodisiac. Polly consigned her old name to the scrapheap and asked to be known thereafter as Caresse. (She assigned her first choice for a name, Clitoris, to her pet whippet.) Harry took a job at the family bank. Each morning, dressed in a business suit, he boarded a small boat in which Caresse rowed him to Place de la Concorde, from which he walked to his office on Place Vendôme. In both directions, the curvaceous Caresse in her clinging swimsuit attracted ribald comments from other river-users, which was part of the point.

Having agreed that theirs would be an "open" marriage, both had affairs with others, while promising never to allow the pursuit of pleasure to impair their mutual devotion. (In that event, they vowed solemnly, they would commit mutual suicide.) Promiscuity became the norm. Guests invited to a dinner party might find the Crosbys still in their outsized bed or an equally capacious bath, and be invited to join them there. On weekend evenings, when the weather was warm, they drove with friends to the Bois de Boulogne, parked their cars in a circle facing inwards, and enjoyed an orgy in the headlights.

Having experienced opium on a trip to north Africa, they became regulars at Paris's most fashionable *fumerie* or opium den, Drosso's, described by Caresse as "a series of small fantastic rooms, large satin divans heaped with pillows, walls covered with gold-embroidered arras, in the center of each room a low round stand on which was ranged all the paraphernalia of the pipe. By the side of each table, in coolie dress, squatted a little servant of the lamp. The air was sweet with the smell of opium. After they'd changed into kimonos, Harry sprawled on a couch with one arm around a pretty French girl. Caresse snuggled under the other. With each pipe, the real world receded a little more. "Smiling, one relaxed and drowsed," Caresse wrote, "another's arms about one, it mattered little whose."

Having taken a degree in English at Harvard, Harry put his knowledge to work writing poetry. This inspired Caresse to do the same, and they decided to produce a book. They found the process of choosing paper, setting type and discussing bindings sufficiently diverting to launch a small private press, called, with atypical self-deprecation, Editions Narcisse, but later changed to Black Sun. As well as their own verse, they published such contemporary writers as D.H. Lawrence and Hart Crane, and commissioned translations of works by Alain Fournier and Antoine de Saint Exupéry. Their meticulously designed books inspired other amateur publishers such as Nancy Cunard, Edward Titus, Bill Bird and Sylvia Beach, helping fuel the wave of inventive new fiction that electrified modern literature.

At the same time, sustained drug use exacerbated Harry's natural morbidity. Memories of the war haunted him. His behavior became more eccentric. Attending the Quat'z'Arts ball in 1927, he let ten live snakes loose on the dance floor. In a year when the theme of the ball was the Incas, he covered his body with red ochre, and wore just a loincloth and a necklace of dead pigeons. He founded his own religion, which reached back to ancient Egypt in venerating the sun. Now "a sun worshipper, in love with death," he ostentatiously rejected Christianity, tattooing the crucifixion on the sole of his left (traditionally inferior) foot and the sun on the right.

As excess inexorably eroded the love that kept the Crosbys together, Caresse started a long affair with their protegé, the young photographer Henri Cartier-Bresson, while Harry took up with 20-year-old Josephine Noyes Rotch. She came from the same Boston society as Caresse but was as jealous and possessive as the other was complaisant. "I am having an affair with a girl I met (not introduced) at the Lido [de Venezia]," Harry wrote to his mother. "She is 20 and has charm and is called Josephine. I like girls when they are very young before they have any minds." He knew his immorality would scandalize her less than the admission that they met without the formality of an introduction. Meanwhile Josephine itemized the tastes she shared with Crosby—caviar, champagne, orchids, the color black, the number 13—which showed they were soulmates.

The Crash of 1929 disproportionately affected expatriates like Crosby who relied on interest from their American trust funds. When his uncle refused to advance him more money, Harry returned to a New York dazed and despairing in the wake of the financial conflagration. Josephine Rotch joined him. After a series of sessions with sex and opium lasting for days, Harry sensed that the hedonistic era they'd been enjoying had come to an end, and with it his exploration of pleasure. He wrote in his diary, "One is not in love unless one desires to die with one's beloved." At the same time, Josephine wrote to her family, concluding ominously "Death is our marriage." A few days later, their bodies were found in the apartment of a friend. In an ironic transposition of his suicide pact with Caresse, Harry had shot Josephine in the head, then shot himself. His wedding ring, which he swore to Caresse he would never remove, lay crushed on the floor. He was 31 years old.

As the Crosbys were the kind of people who took advantage of Jay Gatsby's largesse, what Fitzgerald says of Gatsby's character might also apply to Harry. "If personality is an unbroken series of successful gestures, then there was something gorgeous about him, some heightened sensitivity to the promises of life, as if he were related to one of those intricate machines that register earthquakes ten thousand miles away. This responsiveness had nothing to do with that flabby impressionability which is dignified under the name of the 'creative temperament'—it was an extraordinary gift for hope, a romantic readiness such as I have never found in any other person and which it is not likely I shall ever find again. No—Gatsby turned out all right at the end; it is what preyed on Gatsby, what foul dust floated in the wake of his dreams that temporarily closed out my interest in the abortive sorrows and short-winded elations of men."

~❖~

Footnote. Caresse carried on publishing, though never in the no-expense-spared manner that typified the Black Sun Press, the publications of which, remarked an antiquarian book dealer, have become "the literary equivalent of a painting by Picasso or Braque."

Chapter 14.

FOUR'S A CROWD: GALA AND SALVADOR DALÍ, PAUL ÉLUARD, MAX ERNST

When 25-year-old Spanish painter Salvador Dalí paid his first visit to Paris in 1929, gallerist Camille Goemans invited him to dinner and pointed out a pale man with thinning hair, doleful eyes and a sad, downturned mouth dining at another table. He was Eugène Grindel aka Paul Éluard, a poet and member of the Surrealists, whom Dalí was eager to join.

The vivacious German girl with him was Alix Apfel, known as *La Pomme* (Apple). While his wife Gala was being treated for tuberculosis in a Swiss sanatorium, she shared Éluard's bed, although, as he assured Gala in a letter, their liaison was mere diversion: "going very simply . . . calmly, no exhaustion . . . onanism for two, etc." He promised that, once she recovered, he and Gala would pick up where they left off with painter Max Ernst in their *ménage à trois*.

Men traditionally instigate so-called "open marriages," but Gala was as active as Ernst and Éluard in this one. Born Elena Ivanovna

Diakonova, she inherited the intensity of her Russian Tatar ancestors. Her fearsomely direct eyes appeared to hypnotize men, and her boyish figure disguised a voracious sexual appetite.

Goemans introduced Dalí to Éluard, who decided the handsome young Spaniard might make a promising recruit to their busy sex life. Responding to Dalí's description of the landscape around his home in Cadaqués, Éluard suggested they visit him during the summer, hoping the holiday would lead to something more intimate.

Éluard would have had second thoughts if he'd known of Dalí's deficiencies in the bedroom. His strict Catholic upbringing instilled a deep-suited sexual guilt, on top of which nature equipped him poorly. "Naked, and comparing myself to my friends," he wrote, "I found my penis small, sad and soft." He experimented with sodomy at the urging of the poet Gabriel Garcia Lorca, but without success. "I wasn't homosexual," he said, then, somewhat undercutting his indignant pose, added, "Besides, it *hurts!*"

Although the female body attracted him, particularly seen from the rear, he was so repressed and shy that all his life he achieved satisfaction mostly by voyeurism and masturbating, sometime even in church during Sunday mass. It was partly in the hope that Paris would initiate him into grown-up sex that he went there in the first place. Relying on the city's reputation for promiscuity, he tried accosting girls on the street, always without result. He spent hours in the Jardins du Luxembourg, having been told it was a popular pick-up venue, but was left weeping with frustration at his failure to score.

A friendly cab driver solved his problem by delivering him to Le Chabanais, the city's most elegant brothel. Its manageress, Madame Kelly, intuited that sex for Dalí took place more vividly in imagination than reality, and let him loose in a corridor that ran behind a line of bedrooms. Peepholes allowed him to observe ev-

Gala Diakonova and Salvador Dalí, 1930s

erything that took place within. A few hours later he left in a daze, "with enough," he wrote, "to last me for the rest of my life in the way of accessories to furnish, in less than a minute, no matter what erotic reverie, even the most exacting."

Shortly after Dalí returned to Spain, Gala arrived back in Paris and Éluard alerted her to his discovery. "He kept telling me about this handsome Dalí," she said. "I felt he was almost pushing me into his arms before I even met him."

In July 1929, the couple travelled to Cadaqués with Goemans, his wife, and Georgette, wife of painter René Magritte. Dalí was immediately attracted to Gala. His visit to Le Chabanais had encouraged him to explore his erotic fantasies, many related to infantile preoccupations with excretion. Convinced that excrement and animal odours attracted women, he spent the weeks after his return painting a pair of soiled underpants. The day after first meeting Gala, he daubed his torso with pungent fish glue and goat dung, shaved his armpits until they bled, put on a slashed silk shirt and swimming trunks turned inside out, and headed for the hotel to profess his love. Had he encountered her at that moment, their relationship might have expired in derision and disgust. Fortunately she was taking an early swim, and the sight of her on the beach, almost naked, jolted him out of his fantasy. He returned home, washed, dressed more conventionally, and presented himself at the hotel.

When his friend Luis Buñuel arrived in September to discuss the film they were to make together, Dalí could talk only of Gala. "A fantastic woman is in town!" he announced. He'd filled his studio with drawings of her back and buttocks, often matched with images of erection and tumescence. As Gala encouraged his attentions, letting him sketch her while she reclined on the beach or bent over a hotel railing, Éluard watched helplessly as her interest in Dalí progressed far beyond thoughts of a casual *partouze*. Buñuel too became furious at the way she interrupted their filmmaking plans, until, at the end of a boat excursion during which Gala repeatedly mocked him, he threw her down on the sand and tried to strangle her.

Back in Paris, Gala told Éluard she was leaving him for Dalí, with whom she remained for the rest of their lives. By way of consolation, Dalí painted Éluard's portrait, his tribute, he said, to the poet who, in discovering Gala, "had taken a muse from Olympus." (In fact the muses lived on Parnassus, Olympus being reserved for the gods.) In the painting, Éluard's impassive face floats above a deserted beach, flanked by enigmatic Dalian elements: a loaf of bread, a roaring lion, a death mask and the hands of a corpse.

Following the breakup of their sexual trio, Éluard married Maria "Nusch" Benz, a young German model who shared his enthusiasm for communal sex. Max Ernst moved to America with a new wife, collector and gallerist Peggy Guggenheim. Dalí and Gala also spent the war years in the United States, where he painted portraits of wealthy matrons and confected sequences for such films as Alfred Hitchcock's *Spellbound*. His repeated claim "I *am* Surrealism!" infuriated André Breton, who recognized its commercial motivation and rearranged the letters of Dalí's name to create an apt nickname—Avida Dollars.

Gala cooperated in Dalí's money-raising schemes. When California's Del Monte resort hotel agreed to host a ball designed by Dalí on the theme of *Night in a Surrealist Forest*, she officiated at the head of the table in a costume topped with the life-sized head of a unicorn. A celebrity guest list, including movie stars Bob Hope, Bing Crosby, Jack Benny and Ginger Rogers, sat down to a meal of live frogs and fish served in a shoe. ("Filet of sole?" a wit enquired.) The ball was advertised as a fundraiser for refugee artists but the only artist to benefit was Dalí himself.

At the end of the war, the couple returned to Spain, where Dalí, with an outpouring of canvases, books, films and publicity stunts, proceeded to make good on his claim to embody Surrealism. In the summer of 1964, a young American named William Rothlein drifted into Cadaqués. He modeled for Dalí and, despite five decades' difference in their ages, became Gala's lover. (She confided to friends that the only men who ever truly satisfied her were Éluard and Rothlein.) Dalí encouraged the affair and participated vicariously, since he thought Rothlein resembled his younger self. He even suggested that Féderico Fellini film his memoir *The Secret Life of Salvador Dalí* with Rothlein in the starring role.

Gala drove Rothlein to Rome for a screen test but Fellini, unimpressed, fobbed him off with a tiny part in *Juliet of the Spirits*.

Slighted, the actor angrily exposed their relationship by kissing Gala in public. Dalí sent him back to America, then almost instantly regretted it. As Gala grew obsessive, barraging Rothlein with letters and pleading for a reconciliation, Dalí sent him a poem in the form of a telegram consisting of the repeated and misspelled phrase "I lowe [i.e., love] you stop." But the trio were never reunited. Gala retreated to a castle at Púbol, which Dalí was permitted to visit only if invited. She died there in 1982, followed by Dalí in 1989, ending a love story as strange and convoluted as the art he created.

~❖~

Footnote. After French brothels were closed down in 1946, Le Chabanais auctioned off its furniture. In recognition of the importance of his visit, Dalí bought the bath created for the future Edward VII in which he enjoyed watching prostitutes bathe in champagne, and installed it in his suite at the Hotel Meurice.

Chapter 15.

A CLOUD IN TROUSERS: LOUIS ARAGON AND ELSA TRIOLET

An inscription on the façade of the Hôtel Istria on Paris's rue Campagne-Prèmiere commemorates one of the city's most enduring love stories.

In the creative effervescence of the 1920s, the Hôtel Istria welcomed, among others, Francis Picabia, Marcel Duchamp, Moïse Kisling (painters), Man Ray, (photographer), Kiki de Montparnasse, (model and muse), Erik Satie, (composer), Rainer Marie Rilke, Tristan Tzara, Vladimir Mayakovsky (poets) and Louis Aragon, who met Elsa Triolet here. "Only that which once has shone can be extinguished . . . When you descended from the Hôtel Istria, everything was different on rue Campagne-Prèmiere, in 1929 [sic], around mid-day." Louis Aragon. I Know Nothing of Paris But Elsa.

On November 6, 1928, a tall, quiet young Frenchman entered La Coupole, Paris's newest café, to be halted by the shout, "The poet Vladimir Mayakovsky asks you to come and sit at his table!" It wasn't an invitation one could ignore, so Louis Aragon joined the six-foot-tall Russian, who had just arrived from Moscow. Though they had never met, Aragon knew his stirring poetry:

Too slow, the wagons of years,

The oxen of days—too glum,

Our god is the god of speed.

Our heart our battledrum."

They met again the following afternoon. This time Mayakovsky was accompanied by a petite blonde in a beige *toque* hat, a brown fur cloak and a short black dress that showed off her attractive legs. She was so obviously in love with Mayakovsky that it surprised Aragon to discover Elsa Triolet was not his girlfriend but his sister-in-law. More than 30 years later, he immortalized that meeting in the poem *Eyes and Memory:*

Pass my madness memories oh my years;

And you came in November and on a few words

My life suddenly turned completely different

One evening at the bar of the Coupole."

A few nights later, Aragon and his housemates Georges Sadoul and André Thirion threw a party for Mayakovsky, who arrived with a different woman on his arm. Triolet, who was also invited, was so obviously put out that, to distract her, Aragon and Thirion showed her around the house, which they had decorated in Dada style with green walls and distorting mirrors.

On the first floor, she peeked behind some curtains to find an alcove and a

Elsa Triolet, 1925

large armchair. "What do people do here?" she asked. "Make love?"

It was a defining moment and Aragon seized it, spontaneously drawing Elsa behind the curtain and gathering her in his arms as Thirion watched in astonishment. "She kissed him with open mouth," he said. "I could see what was going to be the outcome."

Louis Aragon, c. 1929

Elsa Yuryevna Kagan and her sister Lilya/Lili belonged to the intellectual elite of Czarist Russia. Small, beautiful, intense and precocious, they spoke French and German from childhood. In 1912, when Lily was 20, she married Futurist poet Osip Brik. The marriage was happy until, in 1917, on the eve of the October Revolution, Elsa encountered Mayakovsky. In the spirit of "Look what I've found!," she brought him to meet her older sister, only to watch, helplessly, as the two were drawn irresistibly together.

Lily arranged for Mayakovsky's poems to be published and staged a reading for family and friends, none of whom were aware, as they chatted and took their seats, that the guest of honor had his hand up the skirt of their hostess and was insistently stroking her legs. The reading was almost as exciting for the audience as for Lily; nobody interpreted his work more effectively than Mayakovsky himself. "If you like, I'll be furious flesh elemental/Or, changing to tones that the sunset arouses,/If you like, I'll be extraordinarily gentle,/Not a man but a cloud in trousers!"

When Lily told her husband they had slept together, Brik said calmly "How could you refuse anything to that man?" Mayakovsky moved in with the couple and became, de facto, a second husband.

A jealous Elsa looked for a way to escape from both a Moscow impoverished by civil war and the pain of watching her sister with the man she loved. She found it in a young French army officer, Pierre-Marie-André Triolet. They married in Paris in 1919 but the relationship didn't survive his next posting, to Tahiti, and they separated when they returned to France two years later. After that, Elsa pursued a footloose literary existence in Germany and France, ending in Montparnasse. At the suggestion of her friends Man Ray, Marcel Duchamp and Francis Picabia, she moved into the tiny Hôtel Istria, next to Man Ray's studio and a few blocks from the house occupied by Sadoul, Thirion and Aragon.

Louis Aragon's childhood was as deprived as that of Elsa and Lily Kagan had been pampered. His mother raised him alone, never disclosing where or even when he'd been born, nor the identity of his father. Called up for military service in 1914, he became friendly with André Breton and Philippe Soupault as the three worked as orderlies in a hospital for victims of "shell shock"— post-traumatic stress disorder. When, in the early 1920s, Breton transformed his insights on mental illness and the unconscious into what became Surrealism, both joined the group.

Aragon was a steadying influence on the erratic Breton. The former's 1926 "dream novel" *Le Paysan de Paris (Paris Peasant),* an almost stream-of-consciousness account of the city, was inspired by walks he and Breton took together. "The localities we passed through in his company," wrote Breton, "even the most colorless ones, were positively transformed by a spellbinding romantic inventiveness that never faltered and that needed only a street-turning or a shop window to inspire a fresh outpouring."

Despite its promising beginning, the romance between Elsa and Louis didn't immediately blossom. Aragon attracted women with an ease André Thirion called "diabolical," but existed in a permanent state of psychological and sexual confusion, characterized by what Triolet's biographer called "a capacity for infatuation and an almost masochistic vein of willing suffering." Having just ended an affair with publisher Nancy Cunard, he was consoling himself with German movie actress Lena Amsel, while at the same time dabbling in the homosexual lifestyle of another friend, Pierre Drieu la Rochelle, with whom he sometimes visited steam baths, known as *hammams,* for casual gay sex. "Just to hear the word '*Bains*' [baths]," he confessed, "brings me out in a sweat."

A few weeks after their first meeting, Aragon invited Elsa to see in the new year of 1929 at a Montmartre club called The Jungle, where wild animals occupied cages around the dance floor and customers sat on balconies above them. She arrived to find only Thirion waiting for her. Aragon had sent him to explain that he couldn't be her lover, since he was committed to Amsel and still hadn't quite got over Cunard. As she struggled to absorb the news, not to mention the bizarre decor, Aragon appeared with Amsel. To find Triolet still there startled him and he and Thirion fled, leaving Amsel and Triolet together.

Later that night, the two women arrived at the house, arm in arm, to announce they'd amicably settled the matter. As Triolet really loved him while Amsel wanted him only for sex, there was no conflict. Next day, Triolet moved in with Aragon, whose life she would share until his death. (Amsel's story was more tragic. On November 2, 1929, she challenged painter André Derain to a race in Bugatti sports cars just outside Paris. Hers crashed and caught fire. She and her passenger died.)

Triolet converted Aragon to Communism, which made him increasingly critical of the Surrealists' indifference to politics. When

Salvador Dalí chose the daily *seance* to preview his latest creation, *Veston Aphrodisiaque (Aphrodisiac Dinner Jacket),* consisting of a tail coat from which dangled 30 liqueur glasses, each filled with milk and a single dead fly, Aragon, to general astonishment, attacked him for wasting milk while children went hungry. (For its gallery showing, Dalí replaced the milk with *créme de menthe,* and, when spectators drank that, with green ink.)

Aragon's argument that the party of Lenin and Trotsky represented the only social movement sharing the same ideals as Surrealism eventually persuaded Breton to rename the group's magazine *Surrealism In the Service of the Revolution* and order all members to join the Communist Party. Once it became clear, however, that the Surrealists' concept of Communism had little in common with that of Karl Marx, Aragon, with Triolet's encouragement, started to distance himself from the group.

The rift became public when he and Triolet attended a congress of revolutionary writers at Kharkov in the Ukraine during the autumn of 1930. At its conclusion, all delegates were required to sign a resolution promising that whatever they wrote in the future would be submitted to the Party for approval before publication. On his return to Paris, Aragon wrote a long poem, *Red Front,* which urged citizens to shoot the police and soldiers to murder their officers as they had during the Commune. He was accused of sedition but when the Surrealists published a pamphlet in his defense, he declined their support, claiming Surrealism was "counter-revolutionary."

The couple scratched a living through the Depression. Aragon, as a prolific political writer and editor in the Communist cause. Triolet designed and manufactured jewelry for Elsa Schaparelli and translated Russian literature, including the poems of Mayakovsky, who had committed suicide in 1930, melodramatically shooting himself in the heart.

The couple married in 1939. When the Germans invaded, Aragon declined to follow Breton, Dalí and some other Surrealists to the United States but joined the French army and fought courageously, winning the Croix de Guerre. After France capitulated in 1940, he and Triolet stayed in Paris, Aragon writing pamphlets, editorials and patriotic poems, which were published in pocket-sized booklets by the clandestine Éditions de Minuit.

As the Gestapo and the collaborationist police, the Milice, closed in, they moved south, into the area controlled by the puppet Vichy government. Almost immediately, their shared commitment was challenged. For security reasons and to make best use of limited numbers, the Party forbade married couples or partners from working together. If Elsa wished to participate, they would have to split up—which she was ready to do. "I cannot allow the idea," she said, "that we shall get to the end of the war and that people will ask me, 'What did you do?' I shall have to say 'Nothing'." The conflict was resolved when Elsa, having made a dangerous journey in bad weather to collect false papers, collapsed on returning to the barn where they were hiding. The strain brought on heart problems from which she would suffer for the rest of her life.

Even on the run, sometimes sleeping rough, and in constant fear of betrayal, they found time to write. Convalescing in Lyon, Elsa completed the novella *Les Amants d'Avignon (The Lovers of Avignon)*. Its heroine smuggles documents and money for the resistance. After the betrayal of her network, she finds refuge with another resistant in the ancient Provençal city of Avignon. They bond over the graffiti that anonymous lovers of the past have carved into its walls. Éditions de Minuit published *Les Amants d'Avignon* in 1943 under the pseudonym Laurent Daniel. It won that year's Prix Goncourt, France's highest literary prize, the first time it was presented to a woman.

Aragon continued to write about Triolet, whom he idealized, creating what some called "the cult of Elsa." One of his poems, *Elsa's Eyes,* became famous.

Your eyes are so deep that, leaning down to drink

At them, I saw all mirrored suns repair,

All desperate souls hurled deathwards from their brink.

Your eyes are so deep my memory is lost there."

Following Germany's defeat, the wartime resistance activities of the Communists promised a speedy rise to national power. Instead, the Party, out of tune with a materialist France, saw its support crumble. How could a one-party system, joked Charles de Gaulle, hope to encompass a country with 246 varieties of cheese?

Aragon's fame and popularity as novelist and poet increased, with Triolet his closest collaborator. The two were informally recognized as the uncrowned king and queen of France's political left. Aragon called Triolet "the intellectual adventure of his life," and never missed an opportunity to acknowledge her influence on his writing, sometimes describing himself as only "the shadow of her thoughts." Champions of her work protested that, in deferring to Aragon, she sacrificed her own talent. She disagreed. "I know that I have done a lot," she said, "but it was done like that because we are made for each other."

~ ❖ ~

Footnote. Though he never entirely abandoned his socialist beliefs, Aragon did give in to his bourgeois inclinations and buy an old mill and farm in Saint-Arnoult-en-Yvelines, an hour outside Paris, which he renovated as a gift for Triolet. Since their deaths, it has become a museum, with a garden dotted with statuary, a library of 30,000 volumes and a house filled with the work of such old friends as Picasso and Léger.

Chapter 16.

MAN AND WOMEN: MAN RAY AND KIKI DE MONTPARNASSE

Each July 14, Bastille Day, France celebrates its political rebirth in the revolution of 1789. When American photographer and painter Emmanuel Radnitzky arrived in Paris on that day in 1921, he found himself recruited into a different kind of revolution as Europe struggled to shake off the paralysis of World War I. In that revival, his love for a girl named Alice Prin would play a small but significant part and make both famous—not under their real names, however, but as Man Ray and Kiki de Montparnasse.

In abandoning his name, Ray hoped to escape the mediocrity that encumbered him since birth. He wrote in a poem:

I'm ugly

I have an inexpressive face.

I am small. I'm like all of you!

I wanted to give myself

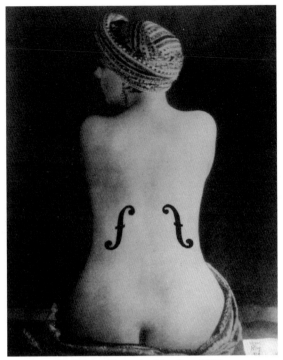

Le Violon d'Ingres, by Man Ray, 1924

A little publicity.

Jacqueline Goddard, one of his models, agreed. "He was not handsome. His nose went all over the place. He always seemed to be meditating, and was seldom lighthearted. It was a great pity that he did not smile a lot. That little grin of his changed him altogether."

Alice Prin didn't share his low self-esteem. "Kiki de Montparnasse" was like a title, acknowledging her as queen of Paris's least inhibited *quartier.* Despite coming from the country and having no education, she felt she was born to be noticed. She was not hindered by not being conventionally beautiful—with wide hips, small breasts, narrow ankles, tiny feet, pointed nose and receding chin Her most beautiful feature was her electric eyes, which artists liked to elongate, giving her the look of a startled fawn. "You have, my dear Kiki, such beautiful eyes," wrote Robert Desnos, "that the world as seen through them must be very pretty. What do you see?"

She had posed for many of the Montparnasse painters and slept with most of them. When work was scarce, she sold copies of the weekly *Paris-Montparnasse* around the cafés. "I get a couple of sous for the magazine," she explained, "but the guys in the back room pay me ten francs to show my tits, so I don't do so bad." She would also leap up on a café table and sing one of the many bawdy songs in her repertoire, demonstrating at the same time that she wore no underwear.

When she met Man Ray in 1921, she was living with Polish sculptor Maurice Mendjisky. It was he who gave her the nickname "Kiki," a child's euphemism for "vagina." Like most Parisians, Mendjisky left the stifling city in July and August. Kiki stayed behind. Even with most of its shops and cafés closed, she preferred Paris to the boring seaside.

Ray was drinking in a Montparnasse café with Russian artist Marie Vassilieff when an argument broke out at a nearby table where Kiki and a girlfriend chatted. Neither wore a hat, nor were they accompanied by a man, and since no respectable woman at the time went out in public bare-headed or without a male escort, the proprietor assumed they were prostitutes and tried to eject them. Ray intervened, leading to all four being ordered to leave.

Hooking her arm possessively through Ray's, Alice chattered about her life as they strolled through Montparnasse. She'd just been working in Montmartre, she explained, posing for Maurice Utrillo. An alcoholic, clinically depressed, with a morbid fear of women, he was confined to an upstairs room in the house of his mother, Suzanne Valadon, also an artist, who, as therapy, encouraged him to paint, though only the streets and rooftops he could see from his window. Working with a model was something new for him—but, Alice continued, when she peeked at the canvas for which she'd posed—well, *putain!* Would you believe, he'd done another street scene, with no sign of her in it! Painters! *Dingue,* all of them. Crazy.

She'd posed for the best: Soutine, Foujita, Picabia, Cocteau, Breker, Calder, Krohg, Kisling, Foujita had a real bath in his studio on rue Delambre—with hot water. Half the women in Montparnasse had dropped their knickers in return for a good soak. Not that they all wore knickers, of course. She didn't herself—too constricting. Besides, it helped when she needed to pee, the *vespasiennes* or *pissoirs* of Paris being designed exclusively for male use.

Ray was mesmerized by this free spirit, without inhibitions, so unlike the women of America. In her fragmentary memoir *Souvenirs,* Alice described what followed. "He told me, 'Kiki, don't look at me that way. You disturb me.' We went to the movies to see *Camille.* We held hands. Vassilieff, whom I didn't know well, was there too. She watched us very sympathetically. Now, he's my lover."

The film they saw wasn't *Camille* but *Foolish Wives,* with Erich von Stroheim as a rake who prowls the French Riviera, preying on the neglected wives of American businessmen. He lures his latest victim to the cottage of a confederate during a rainstorm, urges her to "slip out of those wet things" and courteously turns his back—only to coolly appraise her over his shoulder in a pocket mirror. At this scene, Ray clutched Kiki's hand, and felt a matching excitement.

He invited her back to his tiny studio apartment. Its restricted space invited intimacy but, for that first session, he photographed only portraits. The next afternoon, she returned to see the results. "Presently she undressed while I sat on the bed with the camera before me," Ray recalled. "When she came out from behind the screen, I motioned for her to come and sit beside me. I put my arms around her, and she did the same, our lips met and we both lay down. No pictures were taken that afternoon."

Kiki became his model and lover, and her body, literally, his canvas. The French have no word for "hobby"—only *Violon d'Ingres*, after painter Jean-Auguste-Dominique Ingres, who composed music in his spare time and, when not painting his sensuous canvases of plump, pale harem girls or *odalisques*, played the violin. Ray glued drawings of the 'f'-shaped sound holes of that instrument onto the now famous photograph of Kiki's naked back, giving it the punning title *Le Violon d'Ingres*.

"[He] designed Kiki's face for her," wrote American author Kay Boyle, "and painted it on with his own hand." Canadian memoirist John Glassco agreed. "Her eyebrows were completely shaved and replaced by delicate curling lines shaped like the accent on a Spanish 'n'. Her eyelashes were tipped with at least a teaspoonful of mascara, and her mouth, painted a deep scarlet that emphasized the sly erotic humor of its contours, blazed against the plaster-white of her cheeks on which a single beauty spot was placed, just under one eye."

Ray used Kiki's nude body in every medium, including some erotic short films. She cooperated eagerly. It aroused her to participate, and to see the reaction when he showed the pictures to clients. Her frank sexuality inspired some of his best work, including the canvas called À *l'heure de l'observatoire: Les Amoureux (Observatory Time: The Lovers)*. Like an erotic airship, her giant lips, crimson with lipstick, both seductive and unattainable, float in the evening sky over Montparnasse and the observatory built by Louis XIV.

In October 1929, Édouard Mesens and the Brussels Surrealists appealed to the Paris chapter for help in publishing the next issue of their magazine *Variétés*. André Breton suggested producing an erotic version of the "almanacs" that postmen, firemen and garbage collectors sold from door to door in December as a means of soliciting a Christmas bonus. Most contained a calendar, a list of saints' feast days, a few jokes, and some pious images. The Surrealists' effort, called simply 1929, consisted of some bawdy poems, interspersed with four photographs showing Ray and Kiki having sex. Customs seized some of the books at the Belgian border but many more copies were soon circulating on the clandestine market at, for Mesens and his group, a satisfyingly higher price.

Ray and Kiki remained together for seven years, but the more involved he became with the Surrealists and Paris artistic society, the less she had in common with his new friends. For those who commented that she wasn't very smart, Ray replied tersely that she was smart enough for him, but both recognized that the gap between them was widening.

The relationship ended in 1929, when Henri Broca, publisher of *Paris-Montparnasse,* persuaded Kiki she was sufficiently famous to write her memoirs, which he would publish. Kiki's *Souvenirs* was a commercial success, although it would be banned in the United States until 1970. For the English edition, Ernest Hemingway wrote an introduction, explaining that Kiki was "about as close as people get nowadays to being a queen—but that, of course, is very different from being a lady." She illustrated the book with her own naive, almost child-like drawings, reflecting her nostalgia for a simpler life far from Montparnasse, surrounded by family. While they were together, Kiki begged Ray to let her have children, but although she became pregnant a number of times, he always insisted on an abortion, until repeated terminations made it impossible for her to conceive again.

For a few months in 1929 and 1930, Kiki and Broca indulged in a hot and heavy affair, conducted in the glare of publicity. American journalist Wambly Bald reported seeing them begin a kiss on rue Delambre and remain entwined as they walked around the block to Boulevard du Montparnasse. "It started near the Falstaff and held until they came in front of the Coupole bar," he wrote, "where they were greeted by the little flower girl. Broca bought a flower, pinned it, and he and Kiki went inside."

Succumbing to her own hype, Kiki set her sights on a movie career. In 1929 Broca took her to New York where he persuaded Paramount to give her a screen test. But on the appointed day Kiki failed to turn up, probably having lost her nerve but claiming to have forgotten her comb and gone back to the hotel to retrieve it. "It's for the best," she shrugged. "It's much nicer to go to the movies than to make them."

After that, she was seldom out of trouble. She joined Jean Cocteau among the fulltime houseguests who drifted from villa to villa along the Riviera. At the home of Francine Weisweiller near Villefranche, where he went to indulge his taste for the brawny local fishermen—"Cocteau and I had the same passion for all that comes from the sea," she noted with a wink—he introduced Kiki to opium. Under its influence she became erratic, then violent. When the Villefranche police jailed her for punching a café owner and a policeman, she appealed to Ray for assistance. He arrived with letters from Louis Aragon and Robert Desnos describing her as a serious artist, and a medical certificate explaining her behavior as due to a nervous condition. The magistrate let her off with a fine and a suspended sentence.

Back in Paris, the owners of a club called Babel installed her as its resident personality, renaming it Babel Chez Kiki. André Laroque, her accompanying pianist and accordionist, helped her kick her drug habit. Also with his assistance, she added chapters to a new edition of *Souvenirs* in which she lied about having met and slept with various American celebrities.

Meanwhile, Lee Miller, an arrogant young American photographer and photojournalist, had shown up in Montparnasse, announcing she'd come to be Ray's pupil. He gave in after only token resistance. Miller was that woman whom artists both fear and desire; the Eurydice figure; muse and lover, but also destroyer. She posed for him, slept with him, learned from him, and in time betrayed him. After she left him for English Surrealist Roland Penrose, Ray spent the years of World War II in California, where he married dancer Juliet Browner, returning with her to share his Paris home for the rest of their lives.

Kiki's end was less tranquil. She remained in Paris during the Nazi occupation but when peace returned was reduced to haunting the cafés, panhandling—to pay for utilities, she said, but actually to buy cocaine. Meeting her by chance in the Café Rotonde shortly after he returned, Ray, startled by her obvious ill-health, offered her money. She took it, but, when they parted, stepped out onto Boulevard du Montparnasse and gave it to the first beggar who asked.

She died in 1953 at only 52, and was buried in the Montparnasse cemetery. Man Ray ignored the fact that he had been among those who abandoned her and demanded indignantly, "Why wasn't she helped while still alive? And now the undertaker, the florists and the journalists were making the most of it, like maggots on a carcass." In his eulogy at the grave, Tsuguharu Foujita said that, with Kiki, they buried forever the glorious days of Montparnasse. To the end, she lived a mayfly life with no thought of what the next day might bring. "All I need is an onion, a bit of bread and a bottle of red," she wrote in *Souvenirs*, "and I will always find somebody to offer me that."

~❖~

Footnote. The Man Ray photographs for which Kiki posed have risen steadily in value. An original print of the 1926 *Noire et Blanche* sold in 2017 for more than three million dollars.

Chapter 17.

LOVE ON THE RUN: LOUISE DE VILMORIN AND ANDRÉ MALRAUX

Jacqueline Kennedy called him "the most fascinating man I've ever spoken to." A novelist, filmmaker, politician and archeologist, he was no less a man of action, flying against the fascists in the Spanish Civil War and commanding a tank unit in World War II, sustaining wounds in battle. After the war, De Gaulle made him Minister of Cultural Affairs, a post in which he was instrumental in saving significant parts of historic Paris from destruction. Soldier, diplomat, writer and speechmaker, André Malraux was a man for whom the seas parted, battles ceased and beautiful women abandoned husbands and home, hypnotized by his high forehead, swept-back black hair and the fierce regard of his dark and baleful eyes.

That, at least, was the popular image, which Malraux did nothing to contradict. He did command a squadron in Spain but never learned to fly, and ran the unit according to his own idiosyncratic rules. Asked how to deal with him, the exasperated head of the Spanish Air Force suggested "Reprimand, deportation or, as a last resort, execution." His history of fighting the Germans was equally shady. Never officially attaining his assumed rank of colonel, he led his tank unit mostly from the rear, since he couldn't drive. His war wound consisted of blisters from walking in tight shoes, which were treated by a German military surgeon.

But the woman who became the love of his life, Louise de Vilmorin, was the real thing. *New Yorker* correspondent Janet Flanner called her a "writer, beauty, poet, musician, wit and eccentric, and one of the few gifted *précieuses* of the Paris *haut monde*." Her wealthy botanist father raised her in a chateau at Verrières-le-Buisson. By 1923, she and Antoine de Saint-Exupéry, pilot and author of the famous fable *The Little Prince,* were engaged but she married an American instead, with whom she moved to, of all places, Las Vegas. Abandoning husband and three children there, she returned to Paris, where her father had created one of France's largest garden and plant supply companies. On his death in 1929 she inherited a share of the business and, comfortably rich, set about living in a manner consistent with her taste.

"It was in 1933," she wrote, "at a dinner in the Hôtel de Transylvanie, at the home of Yvonne de Lestrange, friend of Gide, cousin of Saint-Exupéry, that I met André Malraux. We bonded very quickly and it was he who aroused in me the desire to write."

Louise, an accomplished amateur painter, showed Malraux some of her work. He was polite but unimpressed. "Instead of doing watercolors," he said, "you should write! Tell me a story." It was advice he would like to have taken himself, had he not been preoccupied with politics, campaigning on behalf of the Communists against rampant fascism. He was also married to a concert pianist who travelled a lot and preferred living in the United States. He and Vilmorin enjoyed a brief flirtation, like two paper boats caught momentarily in an eddy, before the stream carried them in opposite directions.

For the next 30 years, they met only in passing. Taking Malraux's advice, Vilmorin published a novel, *Sainte-Unefois*, with the dedication, "My dear André, here is for you this book which exists only through you." She produced eleven more, became a commentator on fashion and style for *Vogue*, and wrote poems which Francis Poulenc, who set some of them to music, thought as good as those of Paul Éluard and Max Jacob. They had, he thought, "a kind of sensitive impertinence, licentiousness, gluttony"—not what one expected of a fashionable hostess. Vilmorin put such appetites into her work since, despite her many liaisons, she didn't enjoy physical sex. Botched surgery gave her a slight limp, which she employed as an excuse to avoid being seen naked. The erotic was more stimulating in her imagination than in bed. As she confided to a friend, probably with a shiver of revulsion, "The armed man," i.e., with penis erect "is really very ugly."

In 1938 she married Count Paul Pálffy ab Erdöd but divorced him in 1943 to become the mistress of another Hungarian, Prince Paul Esterházy, then of Duff Cooper, British Ambassador to France. Later the filmmaker Orson Welles was among those who succumbed to what Jean Cocteau called "the pale blue pistol-shot of her gaze" but Malraux remained her great love. She wrote him hundreds of letters, to which he responded in scribbled notes from the latest war zone.

Vilmorin's most famous story, *The Earrings of Madame de …* published in 1951, was the distillation of a lifetime spent observing the everyday treacheries and betrayals of the rich. The wealthy husband of its main character, known only as "Madame de …", tolerates her occasional lovers, while she ignores his mistresses. Having overspent on clothes, she sells some diamond earrings, a gift from her husband, telling him they were lost at the theater.

When he learns otherwise, she thinks she can charm her way out of the situation but he understands that more than earrings are at stake. "I'll tell you a secret," he warns her. "Our conjugal bliss is a reflection of ourselves. It's only superficially superficial." Her failure to grasp this proves fatal.

By the 1960s, Malraux was no longer the unknown with whom Vilmorin fell in love. Rich and famous from his novels and war exploits, he used his post as Minister for Cultural Affairs to block town planners determined to level Paris's ancient Marais district and erect skyscrapers. He also saved the Gare de Lyon railway station with its opulent *art nouveau* restaurant, as well as introducing a law requiring the exteriors of all Parisian buildings to be steamcleaned every ten years. Handing over the portfolio to his successor, he said grandly "I bequeath you a white Paris."

Malraux's flair for oratory made him an ideal spokesman for France. His 1964 address on the admission to the Panthéon of the body of resistance hero Jean Moulin—"Enter, general of the armies of the night, at the head of your dreadful retinue!"—stirred the nation. When, in 1968, rioting students in Paris ignited a strike that paralyzed all of France, with repercussions felt around the world, President de Gaulle fled to Germany, leaving Malraux to deal with what became known diplomatically as *les évènements*— the events—*de 1968*. Once he had done so, nobody was so impolite as to mention that, by firing Henri Langlois, head of the Cinématheque film institute and a cultural hero to the young, he'd helped bring about the trouble in the first place.

When de Gaulle surrendered the presidency in 1969, Malraux took the opportunity to leave public life. He leased an apartment overlooking the gardens of the Palais-Royal in expectation of living there with Vilmorin. Each of them had a floor, with a separate entrance, but they still exchanged letters. "I'm beginning to hate the work that tears me away from you," wrote Malraux. "Don't try

President John F. Kennedy attends dinner for Minister of State for
Cultural Affairs of France, André Malraux, 1962

to lie," she replied. "Work is more necessary to you than the air we
both breathe." He responded, "How sweet it is for a man to have
a woman who understands him!"

Sunday evening salons at the Paris apartment attracted the glit-
terati, including poet Jean Cocteau and his lover, actor Jean Marais,
future president Georges Pompidou, dancer Zizi Jeanmaire and
choreographer Roland Petit, playwright Jean Anouilh, and movie
stars Charlie Chaplin and Orson Welles. In preparation for the entertaining she would host at her home, Vilmorin also redecorated
the chateau at Verrières-le-Buisson, creating a blue drawing room
that was a showpiece of design and style.

Everything seemed set for a long and happy conclusion to a legendary love affair. But two such complex lives were not designed
to entwine. Accustomed to taking charge, Malraux dominated the
conversation at dinner parties, snapping, "Shut up, Louise! You
don't know what you're talking about!" Leaving the table after being slapped down, she murmured to a friend in exasperation, "I

am no longer Louise de Vilmorin, I am Marilyn Malraux!" But Vilmorin was equally guilty. "She resented her own guests turning away from her to listen to him alone," her niece recalled. "Both of them used to be Number One everywhere. Alone, they were bored, and drank too much whisky. I heard arguments. It was very stormy between them."

On December 26, 1969, barely six months after they began sharing their lives, Louise, age 67, died suddenly at Verrières-le-Buisson. She was buried on the grounds, next to a cherry tree, with a stone seat rather than a headstone marking her grave. One might come to mourn her but stay to chat, which is exactly as she would have wished. Until his death seven years later, Malraux continued to live at the chateau with Louise's niece, Sophie. She travelled with him and became his hostess and companion. He had attained the "last love" for which he waited so long; just not with the woman he expected.

~ ❖ ~

Footnote. In 1923, Malraux, his wife Clara Goldschmidt, and an associate Louis Chevasson were arrested in Phnom-Penh while trying to ship to France a ton of sculptures looted from Cambodian temples. Facing a three-year prison sentence, Malraux sent his wife back to Paris, where she persuaded Louis Aragon, André Gide and André Breton to sign a petition demanding privileged status for "those who contribute to increasing the intellectual heritage of our country." Their convictions were reduced to suspended sentences and they were allowed to return to France, and the episode became the subject of a 1967 novel by Walter Langlois, *André Malraux: The Indochina Adventure.*

Chapter 18.

MANIACS OF LOVE: HENRY MILLER AND ANAÏS NIN

What cosmic comedian decreed that burly, foul-mouthed New York-born Henry Valentine Miller should even find himself in the same room with, let alone share the bed of tiny, lisping Franco/Cuban Angela Anaïs Juana Antolina Rosa Edelmira Nin y Culmell? Such a relationship could only have germinated in the rich soil of Paris during the period between the world wars. As Miller would later write, "Paris attracts the tortured, the hallucinated, the great maniacs of love. Here, at the very hub of the wheel, one can embrace the most fantastic, the most impossible theories, without finding them in the least strange."

Neither Miller nor Nin belonged to the so-called "Lost Generation" of literary expatriates. They didn't attend Gertrude Stein's Saturday evening soirées, holiday with Gerald and Sara Murphy at Antibes, hang out with Sylvia Beach at Shakespeare and Company or help Eugène Jolas edit the literary journal *transition*. On the contrary, according to poet Robert W. Service, Miller regarded his fellow expatriates as phonies, dismissing with contempt, "the pretentious scribes of the Latin Quarter and their freak magazine."

Coarse and often belligerent, Miller failed as a novelist while working for the US Post Office but hoped that Paris would free him to write frankly in the realist style pioneered by Dostoevsky, Huysmans, Balzac and Nietzsche. At first, however, the only employment he could find was teaching English in a provincial language school.

Nin too wished to stretch herself intellectually and sensually but was kept busy as hostess for her banker husband Hugo Guiler in their villa at suburban Louveciennes. Seduced by her father, the composer Joaquin Nin, a notorious Don Juan who abandoned his family when she was only 9 years old, Nin looked back on the experience not as molestation but initiation. It left her conflicted about sex but also perversely attracted to its possibilities. She found secret pleasure in goading men to arousal, then rebuffing them and describing the experience in her journal, which she began as a protracted letter to her lost father.

Her indecision was resolved in December 1931 when lawyer Richard Osborn brought Henry Miller to lunch, hoping Guiler might become his patron. "When he first stepped out of the car and walked towards the door where I stood waiting," wrote Nin, "I saw a man I liked. In his writing he is flamboyant, virile, animal, magnificent. He is a man whom life makes drunk, I thought. He is like me." Almost immediately she knew they would be lovers. "Henry was the only one who plucked the fruit at the right moment."

They began meeting in the afternoon, choosing small Montparnasse cafés rather than the more public Dôme and Rotonde. Miller had found a job as copy editor on the Paris edition of the *Chicago Tribune* and was living at the Hôtel Central, just off rue de la Gaité, a street lined with seedy cabarets and *hotels de passe*.

For five months the couple circled around the idea of physical sex, fearing it would undermine their rapport. Consummation was further delayed by the arrival in Paris of Miller's wife, June Mansfield. They'd met when she was a dime-a-dance partner in a Times Square "dance academy." Bisexual, and ambitious to act in movies, she hoped Paris would widen both her professional and emotional horizons. She made an instant impression on Anaïs, who transferred to her some of the passion she felt for Henry. "A startlingly white face," Nin wrote, "burning eyes. As she came towards me from the darkness of my garden into the light of the doorway I saw for the first time the most beautiful woman on earth. Years ago, when I tried to imagine a pure beauty, I had created an image in my mind of just that woman. Henry faded: she was color, brilliance, strangeness."

Mansfield's presence made Nin even more determined to take her relationship with Henry to the next level. On March 6, 1932, in Room 401 of the Hôtel Central, she joined him in bed for the first time. He was everything she hoped for in a lover, obliterating all her fears. As they relaxed between bouts of sex, they discussed literature. She left their rendezvous both physically and intellectually replete, "a sperm-filled woman, loaded with the phrases Henry had given me."

But even while she pleasured herself with Henry, Nin filled her diary with erotic fantasies about June. Hoping to resolve these and other conflicts, she entered psychoanalysis with Austrian therapist Otto Rank, friend and student of Sigmund Freud. Meanwhile, Hugo Guiler, unaware of his wife's infidelity, agreed to support Miller while he completed a novel.

Miller moved to Villa Seurat, in the 14th *arrondissement*, far from the distractions of Montparnasse. An *impasse* lined with modern townhouses, each with a capacious studio, it had been created a decade earlier by architect and *tapissier* Jean Lurçat as a *cité des*

THE·EARLY·DIARY·OF
ANAÏS NIN

*With a Preface by
Joaquín Nin-Culmell*

A Harvest Book

The Early Diary of Anaïs Nin, Vol. 4
(1927 – 1931), 1986

artistes where creative people could find a calm and sedate atmosphere in which to work. Miller changed that when he moved into No. 18. He threw raucous parties, one of which Anaïs attended with author Rebecca West, who loathed Miller from the start, calling him "a dreadful American lout." She continued, "He got very drunk. He tried to take a bath half-dressed and Anaïs Nin and I discovered him under the water, blowing bubbles. We pulled him out, and in the course of this the rest of his clothes came off. I may say that Henry Miller without clothes was even less appealing than Henry Miller with clothes."

Miller's relish for the life of the streets, the more squalid the better, left Nin both repelled and titillated. Hoping to further loosen up the stuffy Hugo Guiler and satisfy the hunger of Anaïs for new sensations, Miller and June took them to a brothel to watch a sexual exhibition. The girls of the house invited them to join in, but Henry was the only one to do so, the others just looking on with curiosity and embarrassment. He also enjoyed using the *vespasiennes* or public urinals scattered around the city, particularly a *pissoir* just outside the Jardins du Luxembourg, where he could urinate while watching bourgeois mothers and nannies playing with their children and picnicking on the grass.

Once Miller finished *Tropic of Cancer*, Anaïs borrowed money from Otto Rank, by now also her lover, to have it published by Jack Kahane's Obelisk Press. The book made no concessions to contemporary sensibility. Miller called it "a prolonged insult, a gob of spit in the face of Art, a kick in the pants to God, Man, Destiny, Time, Love, Beauty." Not expecting that anything he published would survive more than one reading, Kahane used paper hardly better than newsprint and, as reputable bookshops refused to stock his titles, employed a team of shifty individuals to peddle them around the city's cafés and bars.

With her movie career stalled and Henry preoccupied with his writing and the affair with Nin, Mansfield returned to New York and divorced him. In 1934, Anaïs had an abortion. The guilt it induced would reverberate through the rest of her involvement with Henry, tempting her to test repeatedly the intensity of his feelings.

From time to time, they had sex in the house at Louveciennes, narrowly avoiding being caught *in flagrante*. Such experiences only sharpened her pleasure in taking risks. About this time, Henry received a letter that contained an affectionate note meant for Hugo. Assuming she had confused the envelopes and that Hugo had a letter intended for him, he visualized a violent confrontation with the cuckolded Guiler. Frightened to answer his door, he asked a friend to move in for protection. After a few days, the correct letter arrived. It was polite and distant, without a hint of their illicit relationship. Miller realized Anaïs had played a trick on him, and reverted to her earlier habit of teasing men to test the degree of their desire.

In 1935, the Guilers and Miller travelled independently to New York, where Anaïs suggested to Otto Rank that having twice undergone analysis qualified her to practice as a therapist. He was unconvinced but let her treat some of his patients. She in turn recruited Henry to help out, even though he knew nothing of psychiatry. Rising to the challenge, he gave her clients "a little measure of St. Augustine, an ounce of Emerson, a pinch of the Old Testament, a tincture of Forel and Freud, and a sprinkling of Lao-Tse," but quickly became bored, and pressed Anaïs to return with him to Paris. She refused, so he went back alone, completing the second book of his trilogy, *Tropic of Capricorn,* and starting work on the third, *Black Spring.*

On her return, Miller and Nin resumed their affair but bonded as often over a manuscript as in bed, diverting some of their sexual energy into their work. As Hitler invaded Poland in 1939, Miller and the Guilers sailed again for New York, where they remained throughout the war. Nin joined the bohemian society of Greenwich Village. Her new friends included painter Virginia Admiral, her husband Robert De Niro, Sr. and poet Robert Duncan. With them, and later joined by Miller, she began writing erotic stories for an Oklahoma industrialist who paid a then-generous $1 a page. She would later adapt them into her book *Delta of Venus.* Guiler too felt free to exercise the creativity he had suppressed in his work as a banker, and, under the pseudonym Ian Hugo, emerged as a gifted graphic artist and experimental filmmaker.

A few weeks before they sailed for New York, Henry and Anaïs spent some days together in Aix-en-Provence where they shared their last "literary fuck fest." Henry, not knowing if either would survive the war, drafted a will leaving her his entire estate. "I owe a lot to France," he wrote, "but I must add in the interests of truth that I owe almost everything to one person, Anaïs Nin. Had I not met her, I would not have accomplished the little I did. I would have starved to death. It was a woman, Anaïs Nin, by whom I was rescued and pressured and encouraged and inspired."

~ ❖ ~

Footnote. Henry Miller had five marriages, the last to Hoki Tokuda, who opened a piano bar in Tokyo called *Tropic of Cancer,* but admitted she hadn't read the book. Miller and Tokuda never made love or shared a bed. "I kissed Henry just once," she said, "and he was a terrible kisser. It was not romantic. It was all...*wet.*"

Chapter 19.

FRIENDS OF THE BOOK: SYLVIA BEACH AND ADRIENNE MONNIER

I n 1919, the hat of an American woman blew off as she walked up rue de l'Odéon on the left bank of the Seine. The proprietor of a bookshop called *La Maison des Amis des Livres* (The House of Friends of Books) stepped out and rescued it. This meeting changed not only the lives of both women but modern literature also, since the American would remain in Paris, open her own bookshop and publish a novel that overturned traditional concepts of narrative. Sylvia Beach wrote that there were three loves in her life: her shop, Shakespeare and Company, James Joyce, author of *Ulysses,* and the woman who rescued her hat, Adrienne Monnier.

When we think of Beach and Monnier we picture them as middle-aged, because it took a decade for them to become public figures. In fact, Adrienne was only 23 in 1915 when she started her bookshop, and not even 30 when she met Beach. Also, we assume, because of Monnier's good sense and slightly frumpy image, that she was the older, when Beach was the elder by six years.

Beach first came to Paris in 1902 with her Presbyterian minister father, an inauspicious way to encounter the City of Light. "I was not interested in what I could see of Paris through the bars of my family prison," she grumbled with teenage belligerence. By 1914, however, she had acquired the Francophilia of her father who, as long as the United States stayed out of the War, made his sympathies clear by draping the *tricolor* over the pulpit during his Sunday sermon. Some parishioners took the hint and volunteered to fight. In 1916 Sylvia joined them, only to discover that the French wanted only people with military or medical expertise. The unqualified were diverted to ambulance units or jobs that freed French citizens to fight. Beach became an agricultural laborer. After two years digging turnips, she was sent to the Balkans to hand out pajamas to needy Croats.

After the war, Beach had no money to continue her studies of French poetry. After meeting Monnier, she considered opening a branch of *La Maison des Amis des Livres* in New York, a plan which Adrienne, always the better businesswoman, recognized as a recipe for disaster. However, with Americans crowding into Paris with more expected as the economy recovered, an English-language bookshop in Paris might stand a chance. Beach's mother lent the money to open the first Shakespeare and Company in a converted laundry on rue Dupuytren, around the corner from Odéon, then in larger premises on rue de l'Odéon, diagonally opposite Monnier's shop.

From the start, the shop was, in Sylvia's words, a "problematic little business." With only two rooms and a small apartment above, there was insufficient space for a large stock. It limped along on the income from lending books, and even its fees were more than many could afford; she let newcomers such as Ernest Hemingway borrow on credit. At every stage, Adrienne's support was essential. As a French citizen and property owner, she stood guarantor for the lease, and also owned the apartment they shared. Later, she helped Sylvia apply for French government assistance for the shop, rallying some literary notables to sign a petition. When it was refused, Sylvia formed the Friends of Shakespeare and Company. Nonmembers had to pay to attend the readings and other events she staged.

Neither Adrienne nor Sylvia paid much attention to how they dressed, despite living in a city preoccupied with clothes. Janet Flanner described Monnier as "buxom as an abbess, placidly picturesque in the costume she permanently adopted, consisting of a long, full gray skirt, a bright velveteen waistcoat and a white blouse" and Beach as "slim, jacketed . . . with her schoolgirl white collar and big colored bowknot, in the style of Colette's *Claudine à l'Ecole.*" Sylvia, in avoiding overtly feminine clothing, projected the businesslike style she thought appropriate to a bookseller. Adrienne's ground-sweeping skirts and high-necked blouses disguised her dumpy figure, and made her, from a distance, resemble, according to one cynical observer, a peasant woman standing knee-deep in ploughed earth.

They were no less badly matched in temperament. Sylvia's manner was brisk and mannish. She impressed Ernest Hemingway with the almost masculine way she responded to his offer, made during his first visit, to display his shrapnel-riddled leg, instantly locking the door, putting up the "Closed" sign and inviting him to drop his trousers. Adrienne was, by contrast, placid and accommodating. A friend remembered her in her shop, "sitting facing the street, in the center of a sort of pulpit, a fortified enclosure with a corridor for close friends."

She was "spiritual, greedy, expert in fine literature and good cuisine, always pleasant, cheerful, combining the love of books with the love of readers." *La Maison des Amis des Livres* was less a conventional bookshop than a venue for readings and discussions, and a base for Monnier's efforts as a publisher, which included two magazines, *Le Navire d'Argent* and *Mesures,* and a number of monographs, as well as the first French-language edition of *Ulysses*. She supported these not with sales of new books, which appear to have been negligible, but from family money and by selling off her own collection of rarities.

Adrienne seduced Sylvia but the seduction was more intellectual than sexual. Monnier had lovers of both sexes before, during and after their partnership but Sylvia appears to have no sexual history at all. They didn't share a bed; their apartment was large enough for separate bedrooms. Nor did they socialize with Paris's lesbian community. *New Yorker* correspondent Janet Flanner, herself a lesbian, hinted that, as a minister's daughter, Beach disapproved of same-sex relationships. "Sylvia had inherited morality," Flanner said, "and you could feel it in her." Two floors above their apartment, Australian painter Agnes Goodsir and her partner Rachel Dunne lived openly as a couple. Twenty minutes' walk away was the home of Paris's doyenne of Sapphic sex, Natalie Clifford Barney, and, in the opposite direction Gertrude Stein and Alice Toklas. Beach and Monnier knew Stein and Barney but their relationship was distant. Sylvia's comments on the Friday afternoon *coctels* held by Natalie Barney at her house on rue Jacob were brief and remote. "At Miss Barney's, one met lesbians," she said. "Paris ones and those only passing through town, ladies with high collars and monocles." She left it to others to mock the predatory instincts of their hostess, who built a quasi-Greek temple to Friendship in the grounds and used it as a setting for seduction. Djuna Barnes parodied her as Dame Evangeline Musset in her 1928 quasi-Elizabethan satire *The Ladies' Almanack,* a woman "much in Demand, and wide-famed for her Genius at bringing up by Hand, and noted and esteemed for her Slips of the Tongue."

Sylvia Beach and her partner Adrienne Monnier, 1928

Beach's clientele dwindled as the Depression ravaged private incomes. "My business," she wrote, "is suffering excruciatingly from the exodus of Americans." Greater damage was inflicted by her impetuous decision to publish James Joyce's *Ulysses,* which was probably inspired by what Monnier was publishing. Sylvia bore the entire cost of having the text typeset and printed, defraying her investment by extracting advance orders from foreign collectors and dealers. They alone could afford a book which, as one British schoolteacher complained, cost as much as his month's salary. As soon as any money accumulated, Joyce seized it. Moreover, when an American judge cleared *Ulysses* for publication in 1933, the author ignored the fact that Beach still owned the rights and sold them to Random House for a hefty advance, all of which he kept for himself.

Publishing *Ulysses* left Sylvia broken in health and nearly destitute. As she said resignedly, "I understood that working with or for

James Joyce, the pleasure was mine, the profits were his. It was all I could do to keep my shop from being dragged down." To add to her woes, Adrienne abandoned her. In 1935, young German photographer Gisèle Freund arrived in Paris to cover the International Congress of Writers for the Defense of Culture. Among her subjects were Beach and Monnier. It's evident from Freund's photographs, Beach expressionless while Monnier exhibits the smug, closed-mouth smile of the cat that ate the canary, that Sylvia sensed their attraction.

When Freund explained that, as a Jew, she could not go back to Germany, Monnier found a Frenchman willing to marry her and confer French citizenship. Shortly after, Beach returned briefly to the United States and, in her absence, Freund and Monnier became lovers. They would always insist that their relationship was platonic but literary scholar Laure Murat, noting that Freund just as vehemently denied having an affair with Mexican painter Frida Kahlo, observed that "the amorous or sexual dimension is less in question than their efforts to trivialize or minimize it." In other words, if they weren't guilty, why did they protest so much?

Beach moved into the apartment above her shop, although the three remained sufficiently friendly to eat lunch together each day. The American embassy urged citizens to return home as invasion became more certain but Beach refused. Initially she assured her family and American friends, "You know I can take care of myself," ending with a truculent "I am not a quitter," an echo of her teenaged dislike of France. When they replied, however, letters came back "Undeliverable," since the shop had closed, never to reopen.

As Paris became the Rest and Recreation capital of the Reich, it was flooded with Germans of all ranks determined to experience its legendary pleasures. One officer, well read in English, tried to buy the copy of *Finnegans Wake* displayed in Sylvia's window. She refused. It was the sole example of Joyce's second novel to have reached her, and, given the political situation, she expected no others. The officer demanded it anyway, and in the ensuing altercation threatened to return with troops, seize the shop and its contents, and arrest Beach.

After he left, Beach appealed for help to Monnier. Always the more practical one, she summoned friends to Odéon, ordering each to bring a large laundry basket. In two hours they used these to transfer her stock upstairs. Then they closed the shutters and painted over the shop's name. Beach eluded imprisonment, but at the cost of going out of business.

Once America entered the war, Beach was rounded up with other American women and interned, first in the Jardin d'Acclimatation in the Bois de Boulogne, then in a barbedwire-surrounded hotel in the spa town of Vittel. After six months, friends rescued her. The empty shop and apartment became a stop on the informal "underground railway" that funneled Jews and resistance workers out of the city. Among those who used it were Samuel Beckett and his mistress, Suzanne Dechevaux-Dumesnil, who stayed there for weeks before fleeing south.

Beach was in Paris when the Allied forces arrived in 1944, followed by a blustering Ernest Hemingway who "liberated" rue de l'Odéon, but, concerned as always with his image, first demanded of Monnier, "Did Sylvia collaborate?" The war had not been kind to Adrienne, who developed Meniere's Disease, a disorder of the inner ear that causes dizzy spells and hearing loss. She began experiencing delusions and imagining voices, which increased when Freund moved to the United States in 1947. In 1955 she killed herself with an overdose of sleeping pills.

In the late 1950s, American bookseller George Whitman opened a shop on the *quai* opposite Notre Dame and called it *Le Mistral,* after Provençal poet Frédéric Mistral. He bought the books from

Sylvia's lending library, and she surrendered to him the name of Shakespeare and Company. In 1962, she died after a long illness, her body lying undiscovered for some days in the little apartment above the shop that had been her life for four decades.

Beach was too private a person to express her most intimate thoughts but she must have lamented that, of the three people and places she loved most, all betrayed or disappointed her. She gave everything to literature, leaving no time for the sensual satisfactions that France has proved historically expert at providing. "The grave's a fine and private place," Andrew Marvell reminds us, "but none, I think, do there embrace."

~❖~

Footnote. Frank Harris, author of *My Life and Loves,* in which he claimed to have slept with more than 2,000 women, invited Beach to publish it. After she declined, he asked her to suggest a book for the train back to Nice. "Have you read *Little Women?*" Beach asked, straight-faced. "No!" Harris responded. "But it sounds *very* interesting." What he thought of Louisa May Alcott's coming-of-age novel isn't known.

Chapter 20.

LOVE IN HOLLYWOOD: CHARLES BOYER AND PAT PATERSON

For much of the 20th century, the phrase "French lover" brought one name to mind—Charles Boyer. Starting as a Parisian stage star but moving into movies at the end of the silent era and to Hollywood in the first days of sound, he was admired by generations of film and theater audiences as the archetypal Frenchman—cultivated, courteous, seductive, yet never quite at home in a culture not his own. The sense of loss conveyed in his murmuring baritone voice was the very essence of romance. Women longed to comfort him, men to become his friend.

In *Algiers* he was a jewel thief hiding out in the *casbah* or native quarter of that North African city until lured to his death by Hedy Lamarr, the woman who, to him, embodies the Paris to which he can never return. He bantered with Irene Dunne on an ocean liner in *Love Affair*, seduced Olivia de Havilland as a down-and-out gigolo in *Hold Back the Dawn* and, in an startling change of pace, did his best to drive Ingrid Bergman out of her mind in *Gaslight*. (The film introduced a new term to the language: to "gaslight" is to tell people things, then deny you did so.)

One assumed that a man so attractive to women must have lovers to spare but the reverse was true. Bookish and reclusive, Boyer preferred his own company, and was seldom seen with a woman. "He receives boxes of chocolates by the crate," reported one magazine. "Ties, scarves, cigarette cases; enough to set up a shop. He sends it all away, with a word so cold that he would discourage Messalina herself. He loves only solitude, to be alone with his books and paintings, and beautiful music of any kind. This man, who is animated by a burning and hidden flame, is externally cold and even discouraging; a volcano under a glacier."

The few women he chose as companions were generally foreign, looked well on his arm but never stayed there very long. His first adult lover was Renée Falconetti, who would give a legendary film performance as Joan of Arc in Carl Dreyer's film. She was followed by Natalie Paley, daughter of an exiled Russian grand duke, a fashion model who let everyone know she found sex distasteful. Beautiful Czech actress Lidà Baarová drifted through his bedroom before deciding she could do better in Germany, where she so beguiled Hitler's minister of information Herman Goebbels that he tried to leave his wife and family for her. None of these women left even a crease in Boyer's impeccably tailored evening clothes. Many continued to try, however, tantalized by the passion they were sure lay behind his imperturbable façade. "There's a restraint in his *amour*," said one, "which suggests a dam holding back passion that would like to break loose. Women are captivated by such men because they feel that no matter how madly they love, there is still more in reserve." So overwhelming was his charm that, as France steeled itself for German invasion in 1940, the government briefly considered sending him on a lecture tour to reassure wives and mothers that their recently mobilized sons and husbands were in safe hands. The women of France might not trust their president but Charles Boyer could convince them of anything.

Boyer had an equally small number of male friends. One was Maurice Chevalier, whom he met in the early 1930s when the song-and-dance man's Hollywood career was in decline. "At a time when I was lonely and shaken, Charles offered me his friendship," said Chevalier. "I liked him more every time I saw him, and found I could talk with him on subjects that usually found me speechless. Finally we were together almost every evening. I will always be grateful for the friendship of this man."

Boyer's one passion was gambling, at which an exceptional memory made him a consistent winner, particularly at the high stakes poker games hosted by Hollywood's studio bosses. They put him on first-name terms with such moguls as Joseph Schenck, Irving Thalberg and Darryl F. Zanuck, and gave him unique access to the corridors of movie power.

Until 1934, one would have given good odds on Boyer dying a bachelor. Early in January of that year, he arrived in Los Angeles with a group of French actors and actresses. There was a lunch party at the Fox studios a few days later. Boyer knew a few of the guests, among them Spencer Tracy, with whom he shared, at the time, the same rung on the career ladder. Tracy was appearing at Fox in the musical *Bottoms Up*. Also at the party was that film's female lead, young English actress Patricia Paterson.

From the first glance, Boyer couldn't take his eyes off her. That night, he telephoned and asked her out. Anyone who knew the "Boyer type" would have understood the attraction of her oval face and pointed chin, high forehead and large clear eyes. Like other women he had dated, she dressed well, was foreign (she played a Canadian in *Bottoms Up* but actually came from Bradford in the English midlands), was ten years younger than Boyer and, at 5 feet 2 inches, much shorter, all of which added to her appeal

Pat Paterson and Charles Boyer, 1935

For the next three weeks, they were seldom apart. One evening, they arrived at the premiere of Garbo's *Queen Christina* at Grauman's Chinese Cinema on Hollywood Boulevard, to find the film had already started. Rather than stumble to their seats in the dark, Pat asked "What shall we do now?"

Boyer said impulsively "Well, we could get married."

After a few seconds, both laughed, but the seed had been planted. Three days later, on Saint Valentine's Day, they drove to Yuma, just over the border in Arizona, a state that allowed "quickie" weddings.

Maurice Chevalier hosted a reception for the newlyweds. Like almost everyone who knew Boyer, he was incredulous. "I couldn't believe it of Charles," he said. "Why, he could have had any woman in France!" But others sensed that he and Pat suited one another. He would soon have lost patience with a flighty partner such as actress Claudette Colbert, who had been eager to marry him, and those Parisian women who challenged his set opinions. But his friend André Daven recognized their complementary natures. "Charles couldn't help it that he was such a moody person but Pat understood his moods perfectly. She read a lot too, but not the same things. She read bestsellers like *Gone With the Wind* and I suppose *Forever Amber*. She wasn't deep, and he loved her because she didn't pretend to be."

Pat adjusted to Boyer's ways, including his insistence on spending two months of each year in France. Neither was particularly religious but she also converted to Catholicism. She got on only moderately well with his bossy mother Louise, a widow who raised Charles, her only child, alone, and remained protective of him as an adult.

When their son Michael was born, Louise insisted on teaching him French and calling him "Michel." An unhappy child, Michael was both neglected and spoiled by his parents as they pursued a Hollywood lifestyle, attending dinner parties and shuttling between Los Angeles, Paris and their villa on the island of Ischia, in the bay of Naples. He made few friends, and his isolation was exacerbated by a bad stammer. In adolescence he dropped out of school, hoping to work in movies, but failed in the entry-level job his father found for him in television.

Surprising for someone so seductive in voice and manner, Boyer could neither sing or dance, but nevertheless agreed to collaborate with his son on an album of song lyrics spoken over orchestral accompaniment. Although the album sold well, Michael proved a poor businessman. Instead of exploiting his success, he drifted into a life of fast cars, older women, and guns. In 1965 he died of a gunshot to the head, apparently during a game of Russian Roulette.

Charles and Pat never recovered from his loss. They left California to live in Switzerland, but in 1978 relocated in Arizona. For their 44th wedding anniversary, friends arranged a small gathering in Los Angeles. Charles took the opportunity of being back in the United States to undergo a complete physical, and persuaded Pat to do the same. The tests revealed that she had advanced colon and liver cancer. Doctors gave her less than a year to live.

So began for Boyer what one newspaper called, "the most intense role of his acting career." Once he absorbed the news, he had one paramount response: she must not know. He revealed her condition to a few friends, insisting they maintain the fiction of her good health. A doctor was persuaded to write a medical certificate attributing Pat's growing debility to hepatitis. Boyer assured her that rest and a change in diet would reverse her loss of energy and weight.

As she became too tired to go out, she dozed most of the day with Charles at her side. Boyer refused to hire nurses to share the burden of care. "He protected her, remained with her, comforted her," wrote the local newspaper, "made plans for the Christmas he knew she would never see." To maintain the pretense that they would leave Arizona to spend the summer somewhere cooler, he closed their house, moving into the home of a long-time friend, which freed him to spend all his time at her side. They played gin, and he read to her, mostly from the English literary classics she'd known since childhood. Sometimes he read a play, taking all the roles, changing accents.

In August, he started reading Charles Dickens' *Martin Chuzzlewit* to her. It would never be finished. On August 23, Pat spent a quiet day in bed. They fell asleep together, hand in hand. At dawn, the cold of her touch woke him. She had died in the night.

Since they knew almost nobody in Arizona, the funeral took place in Los Angeles. Charles didn't attend, telling a friend that he was racked with pain: the worst he had ever felt. He kept repeating, "If only it could have been me." Later that day, he swallowed an overdose of Seconal. Medics couldn't revive him. At a small private ceremony at Holy Cross Cemetery, Los Angeles, he and Pat were buried under a single stone, next to Michael.

Charles's devotion to Pat gave his later performances a special depth and compassion. Commenting on one of his last roles, the penniless but unfailingly courteous and elegant Baron Jean-Raoul in *Stavisky* . . . , the critic of the *Los Angeles Times* wrote "I've often wished *Stavisky* . . . were an hour longer, so we could see more of Boyer, whose poignancy, delicate mastery and supreme subtlety and grace easily steal the movie."

~ ❖ ~

Footnote. In January 1945, Warner Brothers released the "Looney Tunes" cartoon *Odor-able Kitty*. Directed by Chuck Jones and voiced by Mel Blanc, it featured a skunk called Henri, later renamed Pépé le Pew, who speaks in an exaggerated French accent. His murmuring endearments clearly parody Boyer. Eighteen Pépé cartoons appeared between 1945 and 1962. If Boyer ever saw any of them, his reaction is unknown.

Chapter 21.

BELGIAN TRUFFLES: ÉDOUARD AND SYBIL MESENS AND GEORGE MELLY

Paris's domination of Surrealism in the 1920s and 1930s over-shadowed the groups that sprang up in such cities as Madrid, Sofia, Bucharest and London. Among the most active was that in Brussels, led by Édouard Léon Théodore Mesens, known to all as "E.L.T."

Mesens began his creative life in music and wrote a number of songs before meeting composer Erik Satie in April 1921. In Paris later that year, Satie introduced him to Man Ray, Kiki de Montparnasse, Konstantin Brancusi, Marcel Duchamp and in particular to Paul Éluard, who recruited him into his sexual games with his wife Gala and Max Ernst. Mesens participated enthusiastically, and remained a *partousier* for the rest of his life.

Abandoning music, he embraced the Dada movement of Tristan Tzara, forming a Brussels chapter, and editing and publishing magazines devoted to news of Dada and its successor, Surrealism. He also started dealing in paintings, which would become his primary career. A meeting with Roland Penrose, the British Surrealist who replaced Man Ray as the lover of Lee Miller, persuaded him to relocate in London. With the help of Penrose, he opened a gallery. It exhibited work by leading Surrealists including Max Ernst, Kurt Schwitters, and Yves Tanguy. Mesens also edited *London Bulletin,* an important source of news about Surrealism.

The gallery closed during World War II while Mesens worked as a propagandist, broadcasting to occupied Europe for the BBC. After the war he married Sybil Stevenson, described by George Melly as "about five years younger, a handsome, slightly gypsyish woman with an olive skin and fine aquiline features, dressed, for that austerely shabby time [1948] with fashionable reticence. She had something of the tension of a beautiful bird of prey."

Belgian artists at the home of Victor Servranckx (June 1922); from left to right: (top) René Magritte, E.L.T. Mesens, Victor Servranckx, Pierre-Louis Flouquet, Pierre Bourgeois; (bottom) Georgette Berger, Pierre Broodcoorens, Henriette Flouquet

Then a genial young man in his early 20s, with a passion for New Orleans jazz and the blues as well as for Surrealism, Melly was actively gay when he joined the London Surrealist group, following service in the Royal Navy. He was initially cautious about revealing his sexuality, since, while commonplace among sailors—"On land it's wine, women and song," ran an old saying. "At sea, it's rum, bum and concertina"—homosexuality was a criminal offence in Britain. Also, he assumed Mesens would be hostile, as André Breton had been. He was agreeably surprised to learn that at least one core Surrealist, René Crével, had been gay and many other adherents, Mesens included, bisexual. This led to brushes with the law. Police *agents provocateurs* haunted public lavatories, popular as pickup sites. Mesens was once arrested on suspicion, but escaped with a small fine.

Melly went to work for Mesens, whom he described as "short-ish, plump, neatly if conservatively dressed, meticulously shaved and manicured, his shoes well polished, his hair oiled and brushed back, [with] the look of a somewhat petulant baby or a successful continental music-hall star." Curious about prewar Paris and Mesens' involvement with Éluard and other *partousiers*, Melly pestered him for details. These discussions took place in the apartment above the gallery and, on one occasion, ended in an unexpected manner, as Melly described.

> *Sybil shut her book and said quite casually 'For Christ's sake stop going on about sex. If you want a fuck, George, come in the bedroom.'*
>
> *I couldn't have been more surprised and looked nervously at Edouard to see how he reacted. He shrugged and said 'Why not?' I was to realize, long after, that they must have discussed it before and perhaps that part of Sybil's reason was to wean me away from my total commitment to arse.* [Mesens'] then joined them in bed.] *'You are fucking my wife!' he shouted with fervent satisfaction . . . I was particularly impressed by his orgasm, during which he shouted some French blasphemies and rolled his eyes like a frightened bullock cornered in a market place. And so, high above Brook Street, we made love in various combinations and positions while the light faded, and on many other occasions too.*

The gallery closed in the 1960s and Mesens turned to creating collages, exhibiting at a number of European galleries. Melly widened his circle of partners, both male and female, while continuing to have sex with both Mesens, together and separately. He also pursued a successful career as a blues singer, cultural commentator and arts historian. On one occasion, his acquaintance with the *avant garde* probably saved his life. While touring as a singer, he was waylaid outside a dance hall by a gang who threatened to slash him with broken bottles. He suddenly thought of the poet Kurt Schwitters, whose Dadaist poems so impressed him that he'd memorized some of them.

"*Rakete Rinnzekete*," he shouted. "*Kwii Eee. Fums bo wo taa zaa Uu. Ziiuu riinzkrrmuu . . .* " They turned and fled.

~❖~

Footnote. Melly maintained an active and varied sex life. Film director Dušan Makavejev, glimpsing him in an elevator in London's Soho, wearing a floor-sweeping leather coat and wide black hat, with a woman on each arm, decided his face was "the most depraved he had ever seen" and cast him in his 1974 erotic film *Sweet Movie*.

Chapter 22.

REGRETTING NOTHING: EDITH PIAF AND MARCEL CERDAN

Boredom had a debilitating effect on those detained in Germany's *stalags* during World War II, so French prisoners eagerly awaited the tour in February 1944 by music hall and movie star Edith Piaf. While visiting eleven camps, the tiny singer posed for a photo with every prisoner who asked. It took a while for the Germans to notice that her troupe left with more musicians than when it arrived, and that the photos she took with prisoners could be used in forging fake IDs.

Such visits combined spontaneity and calculation. The Germans encouraged them as a boost to the morale of the guards, who were just as bored as the prisoners, while Piaf's apparently selfless gesture diverted attention from the films she continued to make in occupied Paris and her performances at private parties for members of the Nazi high command.

Standing at only 4 feet, 9 and 3/4 inches tall and weighing only 90 pounds, Piaf never allowed her size, ill-health or personal tragedy to curb her determination. Her songs projected a sense of indomitable will. Stirred by the insistent pulse of the orchestra and the tremolo of her voice, a performance of her signature anthem *Non, Je ne regrette Rien (No, I Regret Nothing)* brought even the most stoic of audiences to its feet. "A voice rises up from deep within," wrote Jean Cocteau, "a voice that inhabits her from head to toe, unfolding like a wave of warm black velvet to submerge us, piercing through us, getting right inside us. The illusion is complete. Edith Piaf, like an invisible nightingale on her branch, herself becomes invisible. There is just her gaze, her pale hands, her waxed forehead catching the light, and the voice that swells, mounts up, and gradually replaces her."

Piaf got her nickname *La Môme Piaf* —The Little Sparrow— from Louis Leplée, owner of the cabaret Le Gerny's on rue Pierre-Charron in the *quartier* Champs-Élysées and the prince of the Parisian night and its homosexual subculture. Having heard her singing in the street, attracting a crowd to watch her father, an acrobat and contortionist, he created the image of a tiny figure in black, alone on an empty stage, which made her a star. With the nickname went a number of legends: that her mother gave birth to her on the front steps of a building in the slum suburb of Belleville, that a passing policeman wrapped her in his cape, that she drank her first milk from a wine bottle and spent her infancy in a brothel. Surprisingly, given how well these fitted her character and repertoire, only the last was true.

Boxer Marcel Cerdan, known as *Le bombardier marocain*—The Moroccan Bomber, and *L'homme aux mains d'argile*—The Man With Hands of Clay, was a familiar figure around Paris as France recovered from four years of war. He replaced young singer Yves Montand as Piaf's companion, just as Montand had succeeded actor Paul Meurisse.

Edith Piaf, surrounded by friends, including middleweight boxing champion (also her lover) Marcel Cerdan (L), sings at a café table in Paris, circa 1947

Cerdan towered over her and weighed twice as much. This was how she preferred her men. A childhood and adolescence marked by privation attracted her to brutes whom she could cosset and spoil in return for a sense of protection and safety. Her entourage had long since ceased referring to them by name, simply labeling the latest incumbent "Monsieur Piaf." Each received the same inaugural gifts: a gold wrist watch, a set of diamond cuff links, some shoes of alligator skin and a snugly tailored blue suit. In Cerdan's case Piaf also set about rounding off his rough edges and inculcating some culture. Dinner guests were startled when, at her order, he put down his napkin, stood up and recited from memory a long speech from Racine's *Britannicus*. "He learns well, doesn't he?" she said, as one might praise a puppy that had mastered a new trick.

Not that her passion was insincere. She loved him as she loved every "Monsieur Piaf," in a sort of self-regarding delirium. "I throw myself into your arms that I adore," she wrote him. "I belong to you, little adored one that I love. Hold me tight against your heart, prevent me from breathing and tell yourself that nothing in the world matters to me but you, I swear it to you on my voice, my life, my eyes."

To have tamed Cerdan gave Piaf particular satisfaction, since he left behind a wife and children in Casablanca. When his wife learned of the affair and threatened divorce, Cerdan snapped, "If you move from the house, I'll break your head!" Piaf shrugged off the risk of him also turning on her as well. Having been raised in her grandmother's brothel and fought other street singers for the best spots, violence was nothing new, and for most of her early career her friends and lovers had been criminals.

Both Piaf and Cerdan were headed for the United States in October 1949, she for a series of concerts, he to fight Jake LaMotta for the world title. He intended to cross the Atlantic by ship but she urged him to arrive sooner, so he took a plane. On October 28 it crashed while attempting to land on the archipelago of the Azores. Everyone was killed.

A distraught Piaf insisted on performing the following night, announcing to the audience "Tonight I'm singing for Marcel Cerdan." She held it together until *Hymne à l'amour*. At the line "*Dieu réunit, ceux qui s'aiment!*"—"God reunites those who love one another," she stopped singing, grabbed the curtain, and collapsed. She was carried off to tumultuous applause.

It was rare for a "Monsieur Piaf" to last more than a year and, had he lived, Cerdan would almost certainly have gone the way of his predecessors. Instead, the singer plunged into a posthumous prolongation of their relationship. At spiritualist séances she attempted to communicate with him. She also invited his family to visit France as her guests. His sons returned home with bulging suitcases, his widow Marinette with a mink coat.

American tough-guy actor and singer Eddie Constantine was soon being fitted for the traditional blue suit but the loss of Cerdan, in reminding her of her mortality, accelerated Piaf's steeper descent into addiction. She had kicked alcohol and morphine, only to become dependent on cortisone to relieve arthritis. No longer able to go on stage without pain-killing injections, she kept a masseuse in the wings to manipulate her spine and joints during intervals.

Eddie Constantine was succeeded by a lover who, destined to be her last, came closest to Cerdan in exciting her deepest emotions. Instead of another bruiser, however, curly-headed, doe-eyed Théophanis Lamboukas, a hairdresser 20 years her junior, had enough of the urchin about him for Piaf to acknowledge that her love was as much maternal as carnal. She gave him a new surname, Sarapo, meaning "I love you" in Greek, and put her team to work making him a performer. The press called them "the most dissimilar, astonishing, touching, ridiculous, irritating, *sympathetique,* immoral couple," but Piaf's public had accommodated her oddities so many times that once more couldn't hurt. In October 1962 they lined the streets of Paris to see her married in a Greek Orthodox ceremony: other churches refused to accommodate the mismatched couple.

Piaf lived for only one more year, dying in October 1963 amidst the same frenzy that accompanied her life. Her last words, characteristically, were "Every fucking thing we do in this life, we have to pay for it." To satisfy her wish to be buried in Père Lachaise cemetery next to her father and sister, helpers spirited her body out of the clinic in Grasse where she died and whisked it to Paris.

A procession of celebrity mourners passed through her apartment to view her laid out in one of her black dresses, a rose in one hand and an orchid in the other, but were swept aside when Théo impulsively opened the doors to mobs of grieving fans. They stampeded through the rooms, helping themselves to "souvenirs." A few hours after Jean Cocteau paid tribute to "that splendid voice like black velvet that enhanced whatever she sang," he too died, of a heart attack, the only event of that day even remotely rivaling in news value the demise of a woman who, notwithstanding her theme song, regretted almost everything, yet to the end kept living and, above all, loving.

~❖~

Footnote. In April 1936, Piaf, then 20, was questioned in the murder of Louis Leplée. Tied up and shot by four men who left his apartment otherwise untouched, not even taking some money in plain view, Leplée was probably killed because he refused to surrender Piaf's contract to a rival entrepreneur. Of those questioned about the crime, most were underworld figures known to Piaf, including her then-lover Albert Valette, a pimp. She was suspected of conniving at the murder but nothing was ever proved and nobody was charged.

Chapter 23.

LOVE AMONG THE EXISTENTIALISTS: JEAN-PAUL SARTRE AND SIMONE DE BEAUVOIR

He propounded the most influential philosophy of modern times. Her writings redefined the perception of women. One might have expected Jean-Paul Sartre and Simone de Beauvoir to bring to their shared love life a rare level of clarity and intelligence. Instead, the relationship was a slow-motion train wreck that lasted half a century and not only disordered their lives but swept others into its confusion.

They met in Paris in the early 1930s, both outsiders from middle-class families for whom the next logical step in their lives was marriage. But encountering new people and contemplating new ideas made them rethink their futures. Both had a roving eye—literally in Sartre's case, since an abnormality caused one to move independently of the other—while Beauvoir discovered that women attracted her as much as men, and was eager to explore this realization.

Jean-Paul Sartre and Simone de Beauvoir at
a fairground on one of their first dates, 1929

Existentialism, the philosophy that would make Sartre famous, asserted that human beings only developed beliefs through experience. Sartre used the comparison of a letter-opener or paper knife, the function of which was obvious. But humans are born with no such discernable purpose. Too many take the easy way out and adopt an existing belief system, political or religious. Existentialism urged them to discover their true nature—their "essence"— by experiment. As Sartre summarized his theory, "Experience precedes essence."

But what of those feelings that seem hardwired into us at birth? We don't *learn* to love, for example. Sartre decided there was "necessary" love, the urges over which we have no control, and "contingent," or secondary love, which we could elect to explore. He proposed a relationship to Beauvoir based on this concept. "Let's sign a two-year lease," he said. They would be married in all but name, with mutual freedom to experiment. Every two years, they could decide to renew or terminate their agreement.

This appeared eminently practical, but proved less so in practice. For a start, the inexperienced Beauvoir needed to explore many options before reaching parity with Sartre, who, though far from handsome and a mere 5-feet tall, was already skilled at coaxing women into bed. "What charmed me above all was the business of seduction," he confessed. Once the lights were out, he was efficient but cold. "I made love often," he said, "but without great pleasure." Exciting a woman to orgasm satisfied him more than achieving orgasm himself. "I was more of a masturbator of women than a sex partner."

Beauvoir soon realized his deficiencies. "He is a warm, lively man," she wrote, "in everything except in bed. I saw that quickly, despite my lack of experience. Little by little, it seemed useless, even indecent to continue sleeping together. We gave up after about eight or ten years." This didn't stop them having sex with others; quite the contrary. Both became schoolteachers, so never lacked impressionable youngsters to seduce. They exploited their privileged positions, sustained by the emotional security of their "necessary" love.

Beauvoir, however, struggled to share Sartre's detachment from "contingent" conquests. "Because we had 'constructed' our relationship, on the basis of total sincerity, of complete mutual devotion," she wrote, "we sacrificed our moods and anything that might disturb this permanent and directed love that we had built." In 1939, she began an affair with a girl named Olga, whom Sartre also found attractive, and pursued on his own account. Beauvoir, loyal to their agreement, didn't fight him, despite suffering agonies of jealousy, and even falling ill with pneumonia from the strain. Eventually Sartre compromised by seducing Olga's younger sister.

Beauvoir had meanwhile started sleeping with Bianca, another of her students, who agreed to have sex with Sartre also, but never at the same time as Beauvoir. As France waited for the Germans to invade in 1940, she and Sartre bickered about who would take Bianca for a weekend in the Alps, until Beauvoir, realizing with whom she preferred to spend what might be her last holiday for some time, abruptly dumped Bianca—and felt only relief. "No more Bianca in winter sports!" she wrote gleefully to Sartre. "We will both go alone to the little chalet." Their relationship had survived its most severe test.

The Germans drafted Sartre for forced labor in Germany but released him because of poor health. He spent the rest of the war in Paris, developing his ideas, which he incorporated into his manifesto *Existentialism is a Humanism*, published in 1946. In a culture starved of debate, the book created a fervor, its concepts furiously argued not only in France but, increasingly, around the world. Beauvoir continued to teach but in 1943 was suspended for seducing a 17-year-old female student and her license revoked. This gave her time to write *The Second Sex*, published in 1949. It adapted and extended Sartre's ideas to embrace feminism. "One is not born, but rather *becomes* a woman," announced its most famous dictum. Such "becoming" was achieved existentially, through experience. Beauvoir rejected all limits on what society expected of a woman, including those of conventional sexuality. "Homosexuality is as limiting as heterosexuality: the ideal should be to be capable of loving a woman or a man; either, a human being, without feeling fear, restraint, or obligation."

Beauvoir and Sartre continued their "necessary" relationship, travelling together and, when in Paris, holding court in the Café Flore or Deux Magots. Both indulged in "contingent" liaisons, Sartre with Michelle Vian, first wife of poet and musician Boris Vian, and Beauvoir with a number of younger women. In 1947, however, during a visit to the United States, she became the lover of Nelson Algren, tough-guy author of *The Man With the Golden Arm* and *A Walk on the Wild Side*. The affair ended in 1951 when Beauvoir refused to marry him, insisting that her agreement with

Sartre permitted only friendship. "It is not for lack of love that I cannot continue to live with you," she told him. "But what you also need to know, however pretentious it may seem, is how much Sartre needs me." She later allowed his letters and her diary of their liaison to be published. Algren was furious. He had been in brothels all over the world, he said, but in all of them "the whore always closed the door."

Seeing *The Second Sex* as an implied criticism of his behavior, Sartre conceded belatedly that his habit of casual seduction suggested "there is something very damaged in me," and promised to cease being an "academic sadist and civil servant Don Juan." Beauvoir welcomed his change of heart. "A man attaches himself to woman," she said, "not to enjoy her, but to enjoy himself." In practice, however, Sartre couldn't resist the women attracted by his growing celebrity. His partners became so numerous that Beauvoir lost count, referring to them collectively as "the family." Always systematic, he scheduled them for specific days of the week, and treated each to the same chilly, clinical sex. One compared him to "a clock in a refrigerator."

It had been Sartre's lack of emotion and rigid reliance on intellect that first attracted Beauvoir, helping her to view dispassionately situations that others resolved by emotion. But over the years, his coldness weighed her down. He never wept. She saw tears in his eyes only once—while he was watching a film. When she told him she had breast cancer, he offered no sympathy, simply commenting that, according to the latest statistics, she'd be dead in 12 years, but by then the world would probably have been destroyed by nuclear war anyway.

In fact Beauvoir outlived Sartre, who died in 1980. When she died in 1986, they were buried side by side in Montparnasse cemetery. Were they ever truly lovers, or simply loving friends, even fellow experimenters? Beauvoir never quite made up her mind but was glad to have been involved with him. "Two separate beings," she wrote, "in different circumstances, face to face in freedom and seeking justification of their existence through one another, will always live an adventure full of risk and promise."

~❖~

Footnote. News of Sartre and the existentialists contributed to the birth of the Beat Generation. In the 1957 Hollywood musical *Funny Face,* Audrey Hepburn's Greenwich Village bookseller, visiting Paris to attend the lectures of philosopher Émile Flostre, inventor of "Empathicalism," finds him to be a womanizing phony.

Chapter 24.

LOVE IN WARTIME: ERNEST HEMINGWAY AND MARY WELSH

London in 1944 was among the world's most hazardous cities, but, for a single woman of adventurous temperament, one of the most exciting. Notwithstanding Nazi bombing raids and wartime shortages, Mary Welsh, hard-drinking, hard-swearing, Camel-smoking, sexually liberated London correspondent of *Time* magazine, found it "a Garden of Eden . . . [with] a serpent dangling from every tree and streetlamp, offering tempting gifts and companionship." Sensing her darting, evanescent enthusiasm for life and its pleasures, Ernest Hemingway, whose fourth wife she would become, called her, "beautiful, like a mayfly," a creature that is born, lives and dies in a day.

At 36 and already the veteran of two marriages, Welsh knew and enjoyed men, and, although still married to Australian journalist Noel Monks, took numerous lovers. Her latest was American novelist Irwin Shaw, five years her junior and, as she informed a friend with the confidence of experience, "the best lay in Europe."

Towards the end of May 1944, she was lunching with Shaw at the White Tower restaurant in central London. Since wartime shortages made new clothes unobtainable, her dressmaker had retailored one of her husband's suits into a figure-flattering new *tailleur,* set off by nylon stockings smuggled in from New York by another admirer.

 As she and Shaw ascended to the restaurant's mezzanine, Welsh noticed a burly man eating alone, and obviously uncomfortable in a heavy wool Royal Air Force uniform. She found his gaze "lively and perceiving and friendly." Shaw identified him as Hemingway. Heavily bearded, he was tanned from the sun of Cuba, where he made his home.

Knowing Hemingway's reputation for getting what he wanted, never mind what corners he cut, Shaw wasn't surprised when he appeared at their table.

"Say, Shaw," he growled, "introduce me to your friend."

London was alive with rumors of the imminent invasion of Europe, and Hemingway, eager to participate, had persuaded the weekly *Collier's* to accredit him as a war correspondent. His wife Martha Gellhorn, a journalist, secured him the uniform and a seat on an RAF plane to London but once he heard she also planned to cover the invasion, he bumped her from the same flight and crossed the Atlantic alone. On arrival, he pulled every possible string to be with the first wave of troops to hit the beaches. Old friends, including combat photographer Robert Capa, lobbied members of the Allied high command on his behalf, but without success.

Welsh had removed her coat in the hot restaurant, revealing that, as usual, she wore nothing under her blouse. "The warmth does bring things out, doesn't it?" muttered a passing airman. Equally

Ernest Hemingway with his fourth wife,
Mary, in Cuba, 1948

appreciative of her *embonpoint*, Hemingway invited her to have lunch with him later that week, "to brief him on the state of hostilities." She readily agreed.

Mary discovered later that the White Tower meeting was no accident. Ernest's brother Leicester had researched those places where he might "accidentally" encounter other correspondents. More flattered than offended, she found herself looking forward to their meeting. It was delayed, however, when, following an all-night party, a car in which Ernest was a passenger crashed into one of the steel water tanks set up around Mayfair by the fire services to extinguish Nazi incendiaries.

An ambulance rushed him to the London Clinic with a concussion and bleeding on the brain. He was still bedridden when Martha Gellhorn arrived, furious after 11 days crossing the Atlantic on a ship loaded with explosives. Ignoring his doctors, she berated him for his selfishness. Telling him she was "through, absolutely finished," she stormed out of the hospital.

Against medical advice, Hemingway discharged himself and, with his head still bandaged, shared his delayed lunch with Mary. Leicester Hemingway noted an immediate improvement in his brother's demeanor. "Ernest was feeling personally admired again," he said, "and life was very pleasant around him." The couple met only twice more before D-Day, but it was enough time to fall in love, and even agree to marry once they shed their current spouses.

After that, the momentum of invasion swept Ernest away. Rather than risk the lives of correspondents too close to the action, the Allies permitted them to approach the coast only some hours after the landings, and to observe from offshore, though still close enough to see corpses bobbing in the surf. To Hemingway's chagrin, Martha, despite lacking press credentials, bluffed her way ashore before him by volunteering as a nurse.

Once on French soil, Hemingway assembled an *ad hoc* platoon of young Signal Corps cameramen and reporters, and set out in the wake of the advancing forces—if not, at times, ahead of them. He still managed to write long letters to Mary, whom he addressed as "Little Friend = Lovely Friend"—later supplanted by the more intimate "Dear Pickle"—assuring her "Small friend, I love you very much," and sometimes ending with an oddly formal "Your big Friend, E. Hemingway, War Correspondent." When another journalist mentioned Mary and asked if Ernest knew her, he ducked the question, but confided to her, "I said yes, I'd met you and you were extremely nice, and didn't add 'And I love her very much and would be glad to show you here on the map how much I love her. But this is only a small map 1-25,000—and I need a Globe and three large Atlases to show how I love Tom Welshes Daughter Mary because otherwise you might not understand.' "

Mary arrived in Paris a few weeks later to find Ernest installed in a suite at the Ritz, surrounded by his entourage, including some villainous-looking Frenchmen of dubious allegiance picked up along the way. Famously, he arrived in the Ritz bar after finding the more luxurious Explorers' Club on the Champs-Élysées deserted by its staff. Noticing for the first time the retinue he'd accumulated, he ordered martinis all round.

In London, his head injury had made Ernest temporarily impotent, so it was only in Paris that he and Mary consummated their relationship. The Ritz, anxious to erase its reputation as a hangout of the Nazi high command and its collaborators, installed her in an adjoining suite. From there, she watched her new lover hold court. It was her introduction to the kind of life she would lead with him, in which writing vied with entertaining celebrities, hanging out with drinking buddies, hunting, shooting, and fishing. Most importantly, she would nurse him through the crises of health, both physical and mental, that increasingly interrupted his work.

Among their visitors was resistance hero André Malraux, soon to become Minister of Cultural Affairs under France's new president, Charles de Gaulle. Malraux deflated Hemingway's claims of feats in combat by quizzing him on exactly how many men he had commanded or killed, contrasting those meager numbers with his own, until one of the *maquis* followers drew Hemmingway aside and murmured "Papa, how about I shoot this *con?*"

In August 1944, Hemingway suffered another concussion. According to Mary, the motorcycle sidecar he was sharing with Robert Capa "rushed into the path of a German anti-tank gun. The three had jumped into ditches and Ernest had banged his broken head, hard, against a stone." Hemingway assured her his injuries were minor. "Am so much better than have ever been since you've known me," he wrote, "that please don't think of me as a hypo-chondrious," but she was rightly concerned.

The full extent of the damage emerged over the next year, when Ernest returned to Cuba. Alarmed by irrational changes in his behavior, he consulted a surgeon, who told him he should have undergone three months of convalescence following his first con-cussion, but worse injuries were inflicted by the second. "A lot of things we took as just unlovely traits were symptoms," Ernest told Mary. "The slowness, loss of verbal memory, tendency to write backhand and backwards and the inertia, headaches, ringing in the ears were all symptoms of what had been done to head."

On the brighter side, he admitted to Marlene Dietrich, a long-time confidante, that Mary was the only one of his wives with whom he enjoyed sex. Hadley had been shy and repressed, Pauline's rigorous Catholicism reduced him to impotence, which he treated by drink-ing goat's blood, undergoing electrical shocks and, finally and suc-cessfully, with prayer, while Martha's gynecological difficulties were so extreme they could only be corrected with surgery.

"Mary was not as classy, attractive, or intelligent as Hemingway's previous wives," agreed biographer Jeffrey Myers, "but she was the most uninhibited and sexually responsive." His new sexual confidence, however, was not without its downside. In his first postwar novel, *Across the River and Into the Trees,* an ailing American soldier returns to Italy and falls in love with a beautiful young aristocrat. The book mirrored Hemingway's infatuation with 18-year-old Adriana Ivancich, whom he met while duck hunting in Italy. He pursued her to Venice and insisted she spend time with him and Mary in their ski chalet in Cortina. Later, she and her mother visited them in Cuba, living for months in the tower where he worked.

Mary hung on, forgiving his outbursts of rage, swallowing his insults and her humiliations. Much of her time was spent accompanying him on hazardous excursions, including several trips to Africa, and nursing him after the inevitable mishaps, which included two plane crashes on the same safari. In his darker moments he told friends he distrusted her and thought she was mercenary. Some cronies criticized her acquisitiveness and obvious pride at being the wife of a Nobel Prize winner. Given the difficulties she faced and confronted with him, none of these seem unreasonable.

His work never recaptured its prewar vigor. *To Have and Have Not* and *Across the River and Into The Trees* were both critical failures, and he increasingly dissipated his energies on journalism. *Islands In the Stream* had moments of brilliance but Hemingway cut one of the most vividly described episodes, the battle between a lone fisherman and predatory sharks over the fish he's caught. Mary claimed to have rescued the text, which became the novella *The Old Man and the Sea,* destined to be his last critical and popular success. Published in 1952 (with a cover design by Adriana Ivancich) it won the Pulitzer Prize and was cited by the Nobel committee when it honored Hemingway with its medal for literature in 1954.

By the time he started work on his final book, the memoir of his life in Paris in the 1920s, published posthumously as *A Moveable Feast* (a title chosen by Mary), his memory had so deteriorated that he needed to phone Hadley in Paris to clarify details. Some people would imply that Mary, watching his declining health, did nothing to discourage him from taking his life in July 1961. While this appears unlikely, there must have been times when, seeing the ruin of the man she met 20 years before, it would have seemed the more loving act to treat him as the wounded animal he resembled, and humanely end his pain.

~ ❖ ~

Footnote. In 1994, the Ritz rebranded the former Ladies' Bar as a shrine to Hemingway, with a bronze head of the writer at the door, nostalgic photographs on the walls and a cocktail menu that included the "Montgomery Martini," with 70 parts of gin to one of vermouth; the ratio of his own forces to the enemy on which British Field Marshal Sir Bernard Montgomery insisted before going into battle. Nowhere is it mentioned that neither Hemingway nor Montgomery ever set foot in it.

Chapter 25.

PARIS BLUES: MILES DAVIS AND JULIETTE GRÉCO

In the period of recovery after World War II, young Parisians, starved for new ideas, were inundated by American films, books, magazines, clothes, and music as Europe struggled to absorb in a few months the products of five years.

Meanwhile, the displaced and dispossessed of the war converged on Paris. Pointedly, De Gaulle designated the Hotel Lutetia, former headquarters of the *Abwehr,* German's military intelligence, as the meeting point for returning refugees. Among those haunting it was Juliette Gréco, a strikingly beautiful girl seeking her mother and sister, deported to the concentration camp at Ravensbruck. Once they were reunited, she became a familiar figure around the Left Bank. Going barefoot, wearing her hair long rather than paying a *coiffeur*, wearing mens' clothes because they cost less than dresses in secondhand stores, she created, through chance and poverty, a style that epitomized postwar St-Germain-des-Prés.

Jean-Paul Sartre and Simone de Beauvoir took her under their wing, even finding her a room in their hotel, the Louisiane. She shared it with an equally lost and beautiful Anne-Marie Cazalis, with whom she was controversially photographed in bed. "Yes, I have loved women—physically," Gréco admitted at a time when such revelations were still scandalous. "You can love a woman as easily as a man. There are people who make you love them, who attract you. And when we love one another, we touch . . . and the rest you can imagine."

Gréco helped trumpeter and poet Boris Vian to transform a dank, unventilated cellar into Le Tabou, archetype of the smoky, crowded, noisy jazz club. Vian led the band while Gréco sang. Her voice seldom rose above a murmur but her beauty and sultry material—one of her biggest hits was *Deshabillez Moi (Undress Me)*—redeemed its deficiencies. Quoting the announcement in a Paris newspaper that "*le petit oiseau noir chante à minuit*" (The little black bird sings at midnight)," journalist Kaye Webb noted that Gréco's "clothes, fringe and unconventional behavior (which includes walking the boulevards in bare feet, and sitting on the curb to rest) are faithfully copied by girls all over the quarter. She sang poems by Sartre and Jacques Prévert in an odd deep voice, infinitely stirring to those under 25 and touchingly immature to those over 30."

Her followers, mostly weekend bohemians, adopted a uniform of black cotton trousers, lumberjack shirts and rubber-soled basketball shoes, the closest they could come to the jeans and sneakers worn by American GIs. They claimed to be existentialists, even though they barely understood Sartre's precepts. Most took them to mean one should live for the moment and explore every experience, a creed that acquired new immediacy in the nuclear age. "One shouldn't look for existentialists at the Café de Flore," wrote a journalist in 1949. "They're all holed up in the cellar clubs. That's where the existentialists—waiting no doubt for the atomic bomb, which to them is so dear—will from now on drink, dance, love."

Losing patience, Sartre posted a notice in the most popular of the intellectual bookshops, Le Divan. "Be advised that existentialism, the philosophy, has nothing whatsoever to do with the existentialism at large in St. Germain-des-Prés. When Juliette Gréco opened the Café Tabou, she was asked who she was. The answer was 'an existentialist.' The press seized on the word. That band of check-shirted youngsters who haunt St. Germain-des-Prés came to be known as existentialists. They bear no relation to me, nor do I to them."

At the Tabou and similar clubs, students jived to the same New Orleans jazz as their prewar counterparts but called it "be-bop," though it bore no resemblance to the jagged, often discordant and angry new jazz created under that name by New York musicians who had endured the punishing regime of the big-band era and survived the war, only to return to an endemic racism that impacted disproportionately on an art where African-Americans were in the majority.

Miles Davis was 22 in May 1949 when he first visited France. A graduate of that world, he had held his own among the cutting-edge groups of Harlem and Greenwich Village but, thanks to his wealthy father, did so while studying at the Juilliard School, one of America's leading music

Juliette Greco and Miles Davis
at the Salle Pleyel, 1949

institutes. His grounding in musical theory would propel him to pioneer the next wave in jazz, defined by the adjective "cool."

His life had not been without complications. In what was almost a rite of passage in New York's jazz culture, he began using heroin, which would haunt him all his life. To finance his habit, he lived for a time off the earnings of prostitutes. "I was a pimp," he admitted. "I had a lot of girls. They didn't give *all* their money to me; they just said, 'Miles, take me out. I don't like people I don't like. I like you; take me out.'"

Juliette Gréco was almost the same age as Davis when the Salle Pleyel presented the International Jazz Festival that revived Paris's moribund modern jazz scene. She couldn't afford a ticket to the Davis concert so Michelle Léglise, wife of Boris Vian, took her backstage, hoping the music would distract her from the loss of her lover, racing driver Jean-Pierre Wimille, who died in a crash shortly after she miscarried their child.

"I lived with the pain of his disappearance," Gréco said, but it was a pain that would begin to diminish the moment she set eyes on Miles Davis. "I saw him in profile," she recalled of her first glimpse. "An Egyptian god. I had never seen such a handsome man. Like a Giacometti." Their attraction was instant and profound. "Music had been my whole life until Juliette," Davis said. "She taught me what it was like to love someone other than music." They had only a few dozen words in common but that sufficed. He moved into her room at the Louisiane, launching a tradition that made the hotel a home-away-from-home for visiting jazz musicians. Her room was rare in having a bath, and Gréco remembered Davis sitting in it, playing music by the artist he called his "darling"—Johann Sebastian Bach.

She introduced him to Sartre, Picasso and the intellectual aristocracy of St-Germain-des- Prés. They walked along the Seine, hand in hand, even kissed in public: unthinkable in the United States. "I had never felt like this in my whole life," Davis wrote. Some African-American musicians, seduced by Europe's colorblind culture, settled there, but Davis wasn't tempted. The music now gestating in his head called for the expertise of American arrangers and performers, as well as an educated audience. He could have taken Juliette back with him, but refused to expose her to the racism that, with the help of heroin, he had learned to endure. When Sartre asked why they didn't marry, Davis responded simply, "because I love her." Years later, Gréco acknowledged the accuracy of his perception. "He knew that black and white didn't go together. He knew I'd be unhappy and treated like a cheap whore in America."

Back in New York, Davis struggled, unable to forget Juliette. He returned to heroin and had some widely publicized and violent confrontations with the police. "I lost my sense of discipline," he said, "lost my sense of control over my life, and started to drift." When Juliette was booked to perform at New York's Waldorf Astoria hotel, Davis, who had never heard her sing, attended the show. Later they dined in her suite, a provocative act in racist America. Gréco recalled, "The butler's face when he entered was . . . indescribable! He took our order, but it wasn't served for another two hours. When it arrived, the dishes were almost thrown at us. Miles called me back at four in the morning, in a state. 'I never want to see you here again. In this country, such a relationship is impossible!' " Gréco concurred. "There, his color struck me with extreme violence, whereas in Paris I hadn't even noticed that he was black!"

Davis's intricate and introspective music brought new popularity to jazz; his 1959 *Kind of Blue* became the most successful jazz album of all time. Gréco drifted into the movies. Jean Cocteau gave her a small role in *Orphée,* where she caught the eye of Darryl Zanuck, president of Twentieth Century Fox. He put her under contract, made her his mistress and featured her in some of the films Fox produced in France, but when he tried to relaunch her in

Hollywood she revolted against the studio's publicity and casting regime. "I am a totally wild animal," she told him. "Do not try to lock me up, even in a golden cage."

Though Gréco and Davis each married three times, he remained the love of her life. "Between Miles and me it was a superb love story," she said. "We never lost touch with each other. When he was on tour, he sent me little notes from the European countries he visited. 'I was there,' they said. 'Where were you?' He came to see me at my house a few months before his death. He was sitting in the living room. As I came in, he didn't turn around but I heard his laughter . . . demonic! I asked him the reason: 'In any place in the world,' he answered me, 'even if I couldn't see you, I would know that it was you.' "

~ ❖ ~

Footnote: In interviews, Juliette always gave the impression that their relationship ended after the Waldorf debacle, but in fact it revived whenever Miles was in Europe. "We were lovers for many years," he confirmed towards the end of his life. In particular they reunited in 1957 when Louis Malle asked Davis to provide a sound track for his film *Ascenseur pour l'échafaud (Lift to the Scaffold)*. Instead of writing music, Davis and four local musicians improvised while watching a screening, an audacious experiment that produced a memorable score.

Chapter 26.

STAR-CROSSED: JEAN SEBERG AND ROMAIN GARY

Twenty-year-old actress Jean Seberg met author and diplomat Romain Gary in 1961. Twenty-four years her senior, he was the French Consul in Los Angeles. Within a few months, they were sharing an apartment on the Ile St. Louis in Paris, where Seberg, after a false start in Hollywood, had just enjoyed her first success in Jean-Luc Godard's *Au Bout de Souffle (Breathless)*. Her portrayal of the free-living American girl who sells copies of the *Herald Tribune* on the Champs-Élysées and becomes involved with gangster fantasist Jean-Paul Belmondo made her an icon overnight, inspiring François Truffaut to call her "the best actress in Europe."

But Seberg's confidence never recovered from her experience with the tyrannical Otto Preminger, who directed her first two films, *Saint Joan* and *Bonjour Tristesse*. Subsequent roles exploited her *gamine* charm but exposed a meager talent. "I am the greatest example of a very real fact," she confessed, "that all the publicity in the world will not make you a movie star if you are not also an actress."

Jean Seberg and Romain Gary

Romain Gary, loud, bearded and glowering, trailing a reputation as resistance fighter and novelist, remade himself repeatedly, playing what one critic called a "picaresque game of mul-
tiple identities." Writing at various times as Fosco Sinibaldi and
Shatan Bogat, and claiming to be the son of Russian actor Ivan
Mosjoukine, he was actually born Roman Kacew in Lithuania.
"Fluent in six languages," wrote cultural critic Adam Gopnik, "he
passed punningly from one to the other in a dazzling display of
instinctive interlineation."

At the fall of France in 1940 he left the diplomatic service to
join Charles de Gaulle's exile government in London, and flew
in bombers with the Free French. While in Britain, he changed
his surname to Gary. "'*Gari*' in Russian means 'burn!'," he explained. "I want to test myself, a trial by fire." After the war he
resumed his career as a novelist. His 1956 *Les Racines du Ciel (The
Roots of Heaven)* articulated a compulsion to live always on his own
terms. Its main character, confined in a German prison camp, hal-
lucinates about the elephant as a symbol of freedom and, on his

release, devotes himself to saving them from extinction. "Think about elephants riding free through Africa," he says. "Hundreds and hundreds of wonderful animals that no walls nor barbed wire can contain, crossing vast spaces and crushing everything in their path, with nothing able to stop them. What freedom!"

In Paris, Gary held court in fashionable Brasserie Lipp and was a familiar face on television, often in spirited defense of President de Gaulle, whom he continued to admire once he became president. When the Quai d'Orsay handed him the plum posting to Los Angeles, perhaps in recognition of that support, his wife, writer Lesley Blanch, declined to join him, so Gary, abandoning both her and his "official mistress," British novelist Elizabeth Jane Howard, went alone. Once installed in the consulate, with his secretary as paramour, he rented a separate apartment as a writing retreat and love nest for his many affairs, culminating in that with Seberg.

Gary and Seberg became a golden couple. They dined with the Kennedys and lunched with de Gaulle. Seberg used her celebrity to campaign for social causes. On a flight from Paris to Los Angeles in 1968, she met Allen Donaldson who, as Hakim Jamal, led the Organization of African-American Unity, a splinter group of the Black Panthers. As they parted, Seberg created a furor by giving the Panthers' raised fist salute in full view of the press. In 1969 she hosted a Hollywood fundraiser for the group, attended by Jane Fonda, Vanessa Redgrave, Paul Newman and other *engagé* personalities. She and Donaldson also became lovers.

Dissatisfied with the films made from his books, Gary decided to direct one himself, and shot *Birds in Peru* with Seberg in the starring role. "Oh yes, she has a lovely face," critic Roger Ebert wrote of her less-than-inspired performance. "We see it for minutes on end in *Birds in Peru*. Looking up at us, down at us, away, in profile, turning toward, blank, fearful, seductive, nihilistic. It would almost seem that the face was Romain Gary's reason for making the movie. So that with a camera he could worship the face of his wife." While on location, Seberg began an affair with Carlos Navarra, described as "a Third World adventurer." Shortly after, on the musical *Paint Your Wagon,* she also shared the bed of costar Clint Eastwood. Furious and humiliated at this news, Gary challenged Eastwood to a duel and booked a flight to the film's location in Baker, Oregon. The actor fled back to Los Angeles and Gary sued for divorce.

Seberg became pregnant by Navarra after filming *Paint Your Wagon* ended. Meanwhile, her political activism attracted the attention of the FBI, which targeted her in a smear campaign, leaking news of her pregnancy to the *Los Angeles Times* and implying that a Black Panther was the father. Seberg attempted suicide, inducing the premature birth of a daughter, who died two days later. Gary loyally announced the child was his, and arranged for the body to be displayed in an open coffin, to show that she was white.

Seberg would never recover from the death of her child. Abusing alcohol and amphetamines, she suffered periods of depression, and made a number of suicide attempts, often on the anniversary of her daughter's death. In response, Gary wrote *Chien Blanc (White Dog),* parodying Hollywood personalities who embraced fashionable political causes and attacking the cynical activists who exploited them.

In 1972, Seberg married Dennis Berry, filmmaker and son of blacklisted director John Berry, with whom she became further involved in radical politics. François Truffaut tried to cast her to type as the troubled English actress in *La Nuit Americain (Day For Night),* his celebration of filmmaking, but she ignored his approaches. Her downward spiral continued. She started divorce proceedings against Barry but before they were complete entered a bigamous marriage with Ahmed Hasni, described as "an Algerian mythomaniac linked to drug trafficking."

In 1979, Seberg went to Guyana to shoot *La Légion saute sur Kolwezi (Operation Leopard)* but was too strung out to work and was replaced by Mimsy Farmer. It was the last hope of reviving her film career. On her return to Paris, she once more attempted suicide, this time by throwing herself in front of a Metro train. In August of that year, Hasni reported that she had wandered away from their home, dazed, carrying a bottle of water, and naked except for a blanket. Police found her ten days later, dead from an amphetamine overdose in the back of her car.

Her death left Romain Gary profoundly depressed. The following December, he lunched with his publisher, then returned to the apartment on rue du Bac he had shared with Seberg, and shot himself. His suicide note, headed "For the press," began "D-Day. *Nothing to do with Jean Seberg.* Devotees of the broken heart are requested to look elsewhere . . .So why? . . . I have at last said all I have to say." Few were convinced. "Both died by their own hands," wrote Adam Gopnik of this star-crossed couple, "though in a way each died by the other's."

~ ❖ ~

Footnote. Romain Gary's novel, *The Roots of Heaven,* was awarded France's most prestigious literary prize, the Prix Goncourt, which no writer can win more than once—a fact that Gary took as a challenge. In 1975, when Émile Ajar won for *La Vie devant soi (The Life Ahead)*, Gary revealed with glee that the book was his, and the man giving interviews as Ajar was his cousin.

Chapter 27.

I LOVE YOU...NEITHER DO I: SERGE GAINSBOURG AND JANE BIRKIN

The Christmas 1974 issue of *Lui,* France's equivalent of *Playboy,* avoided the cliché cover of a glamor girl in a Santa hat and a smile. Instead, a languishing young woman stared out in unseasonal despair below the headline *"Noël avec Jane Birkin."* Photos within showed her imprisoned in a cell-like room, wearing only black stockings and high heels, and handcuffed to a bare, battered iron bed.

That Birkin, an actress of modest gifts and, at least by *Lui*'s standards, an unremarkable body, should enjoy such celebrity had less to do with talent or beauty than with her personal life, which she shared with one of those individuals the French call *monstres sacrés*—sacred monsters. In an added attraction, her lover, the singer/songwriter/actor/director and all-round *enfant terrible* Serge Gainsbourg, not only conceived the photographs but also wrote their somewhat gloating captions.

Birkin didn't protest at being exposed in images that, a few decades before, were seen only on postcards sold only in the alleys of Pigalle. Far from it—she described the project as an act of love, a celebration of the contradictory emotions at the heart of her rapport with Gainsbourg.

Such relationships were familiar to the French, as were men like Gainsbourg—overbearing, unshaven, unwashed, untidy, rude. Literature was full of them. Among the most potent advertisements for bohemian Paris during the *belle époque* had been George du Maurier's 1894 novel *Trilby*. Its heroine, the innocent Trilby O'Ferrall, is hypnotized into becoming a great singer by a "well-featured but sinister man of Jewish aspect" who calls himself Svengali. Far from glamorizing him, du Maurier emphasizes his repulsiveness. "He was very shabby and dirty, and wore a red béret and a large velveteen cloak, with a big metal clasp at the collar. His thick, heavy, languid, lustreless black hair fell down behind his ears on to his shoulders, in that musician-like way that is so offensive to the normal Englishman. He had bold, brilliant black eyes, with long, heavy lids, a thin, sallow face, and a beard of burnt-up black which grew almost from his under eyelids; and over it his mustache, a shade lighter, fell in two long spiral twists."

Trilby romanticized *la vie de boheme* as *Dracula* promoted the erotic lure of vampirism. Social historian Luc Santé suggests that du Maurier's book "affected the habits of American youth, particularly young women, who derived from it the courage to call themselves artists and 'bachelor girls,' to smoke cigarettes and drink Chianti." Under its influence, they looked to Paris to satisfy that perverse desire for degradation the French call *nostalgie de la boue*, a hunger for the mud—an attraction to the crude, vulgar and degrading. Romantic novelists Marie Corelli, Ouida and E.M. Hull further exploited it. In the film of Hull's *The Sheik,* Rudolph Valentino as Ahmed ben Hassan—handsome and, of course, Paris-educated—kidnaps an English aristocrat and takes her to

LP, Jane Birkin/Serge Gainsbourg

his desert camp. When she quavers "Why have you brought me here?" and he responds *"Mon dieu!* Are you not woman enough to know?", audiences, both male and female, shivered—not in fear, but anticipation.

Birkin met Gainsbourg in 1968 on the set of her first French film, *Slogan*, but there was initially no rapport. At 22, she was the archetypal English "dolly bird," coltish, skinny, given to nibbling a plump lower lip and tossing hair out of her eyes. Gainsbourg, 22 years older, had a reputation as a *tombeur*—a seducer. He had wanted Marisa Berenson for Birkin's role, and made his displeasure evident. "I found him complicated and arrogant during filming," Birkin said. "He showed me no kindness; he made me very uncomfortable." But that impression didn't last. "In a single evening," she said, "his character changed radically and I had fallen in love with him." When shooting ended, the two went to a hotel room but, instead of having sex, put on a record and danced the night away.

Sex, however, soon took center stage in their liaison. Gainsbourg had just ended an affair with actress Brigitte Bardot, with whom he recorded *Je T'aime . . .moi non plus (I Love You . . . Neither Do I)*, an imagined dialogue, murmured against a muted musical background, between two people on the brink of mutual orgasm. "You are the wave," she whispers. "I am the naked island." He responds "Like the undecided wave/I go, I go and I come . . . *entre vos reins*": literally "in your kidneys," which an English translator, after toying with "into your guts," rendered as "between your loins," before censors dictated a less provocative *"entre vos seins"*—"between your breasts."

To record it, Bardot and Gainsbourg squeezed into a small glass booth, their closeness amplifying the steaminess of the interpretation, but after her husband, millionaire businessman Gunter Sachs, heard the recording, Bardot begged Gainsbourg not to release it. "This song is yours," he reassured her. "I will never record it with anyone else." The promise survived only until he met Birkin, with whom he made an even more incendiary version. The first reaction of Gainsbourg's record company was, "They'll *never* let that on the air!" But its commercial possibilities soon persuaded them. "Well, if I am to go to prison," sighed an executive, "it might as well be for a whole album, not just a single." The resulting LP, *Jane Birkin/Serge Gainsbourg,* was a hit.

All Anglo-Saxon countries banned *Je t'aime . . . moi, non plus.* So, however, did more liberal Spain, Portugal, Brazil and Sweden. In Italy, the Pope called for its suppression and the state radio and TV refused to play it, rating the recording "obscene and intolerable." The furor left Birkin and Gainsbourg unmoved. They were in love, and by now expecting a child.

With Gainsbourg's encouragement, Birkin blossomed as an actress, her schoolgirl gawkiness a piquant contrast to more voluptuous competitors such as Romy Schneider and Mireille Darc. They never married but lived together until 1980, Birkin initially accommodating Gainsbourg's heavy smoking and drinking, as well as his aversion to shaving and bathing.

As his alcohol consumption increased, however, he became physically violent. Following a near-fatal heart attack just after the birth of their daughter Charlotte, he periodically assumed the character of an alter ego called Gainsbarre. The public appearances of Gainsbarre, unshaven, in dark glasses, usually drunk, with a smoking Gitane in hand, were always scandalous. In this persona he offended sensibilities everywhere by recording a reggae version of France's national anthem, protested his high taxes by burning a 500 franc note on TV and, in his most notorious manifestation, while appearing with singer Whitney Houston on a talk show, announced to the national audience, "I want to fuck her." For Birkin, this was too much. "I could live with Gainsbourg," she announced as she left their Paris home, "but not Gainsbarre."

Gainsbourg repaired their relationship but they never again lived together. When Charlotte was 13, however, she and her father made a record that aroused even more controversy than *Je t'aime . . .moi, non plus*. For *Lemon Incest* they whispered and murmured, to the background of a Chopin *étude*, an intimate conversation that implied a sexual relationship. "The love we'll never make together," growled Gainsbourg, "is the most beautiful, the most violent, the purest, the most intoxicating." He called his daughter an "exquisite sketch; delicious child; my flesh and my blood." Many noticed similarities to the opening sentence of Vladimir Nabokov's *Lolita:* "Lolita, light of my life, fire of my loins. My sin, my soul . . . ," particularly since Charlotte was, at the time, almost exactly the age of Nabokov's "nymphet." An adult Charlotte, who became a successful actress, called *Lemon Incest* "an innocent declaration of love from a father to his daughter," but a critic described it as "insanely perverse." All agreed it was Gainsbarre at his inflammatory best and worst.

When Gainsbourg died in 1991, Birkin, her acting career waning, found a new audience as the guardian of his legacy. She recorded the songs he had written for her and sang them in a series of sold-out concerts. As well as appearing frequently on television, she published her memoirs and diaries, and toured the world, performing his work while Gainsbourg/Gainsbarre joined Svengali and Count Dracula in the pantheon of the unsavory.

~❖~

Footnote. The former home of Gainsbourg and Birkin occupies two addresses in the same Paris street: 5 *bis* and 14 rue de Verneuil, in the seventh *arrondissement,* both easily identifiable from the graffiti-decorated outer wall. The first was Gainsbourg's home between 1969 and 1991. The second now houses a museum, a bookstore and a combined piano bar, restaurant and performance space—called, inevitably, Le Gainsbarre.

Chapter 28.

O, DEAR: PAULINE RÉAGE AND JEAN PAULHAN

Anyone strolling in central Paris around 1954 might have noticed a black Citroën *traction avant* with a quietly attractive woman in middle age at the wheel and an older man as her passenger. From time to time she would park in a secluded side street or along the banks of the Seine, take a school exercise book from her handbag and read aloud to him from a neatly hand-written text. Most who saw them shrugged and passed on. None suspected they were seeing the creation of a significant literary work that was also a selfless act of love.

Anne Desclos was 47 in 1954 and her companion, Jean Paulhan, had just turned 70. Both worked for the prestigious literary magazine *Nouvelle Revue Française,* Paulhan as editor, Desclos, under the name Dominique Aury, as his deputy and one of his principal writers.

For most of that time they'd been lovers. Lately, however, Desclos had noticed Paulhan's sexual enthusiasm cooling. How to revive it? She was not the kind of woman to employ the undig-

Pauline Réage

nified recourse of many mistresses in this situation—sex toys, perfume and provocative lingerie. But Paulhan was a man of letters. Might the literary equivalent be even more effective? Accordingly, she started work on an erotic novel.

After centuries in the shadows, the works of Donatien Alphonse François, Marquis de Sade, had just been reprinted by young Paris editor Jean-Jacques Pauvert. At the same time, Simone de Beauvoir published the provocative essay *Must We Burn Sade?* While acknowledging that Sade was a sexual psychopath who spent most of his life in mental hospitals, she reminded readers that he was also a gifted writer with original ideas about the nature of Man. What were the limits of free will, Sade asked. Did it excuse doing violence to others, and to one's self? The greater our willingness to embrace violence, he argued, the greater the proof of our nature as rational beings.

Sade interested Paulhan, both as philosopher and eroticist, so Desclos took his work as her inspiration. Her novel was a series of episodes in the life of Odile, a contemporary woman, referred to only as O, who, out of love for a man, René, agrees to submit to abuses similar to those inflicted on Sade's heroines. He delivers her to a chateau in the Paris satellite of Roissy where she is systematically raped, whipped, pierced and branded for the pleasure of some wealthy dilettantes, and with the assistance of other women sharing the same willing servitude.

Thus "trained," she returns to her profession as a fashion photographer, in which she cooperates with the group in seducing Jacqueline, her favourite model, and recruiting her for the Roissy experience. O also acquiesces when René sends her to become the sexual slave of a British aristocrat, Sir Stephen. A young man falls in love with her, but she destroys his romantic fantasies by exhibiting herself to him while being brutalized. She is also paraded at a formal ball, naked except for high-heeled shoes and a mask imitating the head of an owl. With each new degradation, O, paradoxically, feels more free. "You made me healthy and happy," she tells René, "and a thousand times more alive."

Desclos couldn't simply hand her texts over to Paulhan to browse at leisure. Her voice reading them was integral to the effect of what was, after all, a kind of pillow book. Fortunately for her, Paulhan never learned to drive, and their business trips around the city with her at the wheel provided the perfect opportunity to dole out her work, keeping him as eager for the next episode as the audience of a movie cliffhanger.

The book both stimulated and flattered Paulhan. Later he would describe it as "the most ardent love letter any man has ever received." It had the desired effect of re-igniting their affair, but also engaged his instincts as an editor. Desclos included a long section explaining the origin of the Roissy group, involving O in a thriller-like narrative, rich with intrigue and murder. Paulhan urged her to

Jean Paulhan

cut it. No breath of reality should disturb the hermetic isolation of O's world.

Réage's journalistic style contributed to the dispassionate nature of the narrative. The feverish language of conventional erotica was absent. Readers became involved in O's thoughts, and her precise reaction to each new test of endurance.

Paulhan also persuaded her to publish the story, and closed a deal on her behalf with Sade publisher Pauvert. Aware that, if badly received, the book could destroy her reputation, Desclos invented yet another *nom de plume*, Pauline Réage. Paulhan contributed an introduction but otherwise disguised his role in the book's composition. To the surprise of Desclos and Paulhan and the delight of Pauvert, *Histoire d'O (The Story of O)* was an immediate commercial and critical success, not only selling well but winning the Prix des Deux Magots, presented by Paris's leading literary café to honor adventurous new fiction.

Deleting its backstory encouraged the search for a hidden agenda in O. Might its rituals and O's elated servitude refer to the benign tyranny of the Catholic church? Others saw it as a metaphor for the Nazi occupation, with O as France surrendering with masochistic pleasure to her oppressors, and the recruitment of Jacqueline a coded reference to collaboration.

Sororal groups appeared around the world, meeting to celebrate and replicate incidents from the book. Elements of bondage became common in *haute couture,* a trend celebrated by photographer Helmut Newton. Labial rings appeared on the menu of body piercings, particularly after Sammy Davis Jr. presented such an accessory (in diamond-studded platinum) to X-rated movie star Marilyn Chambers.

Histoire d'O accelerated recognition of the *partouze*. Everyone had heard stories of such activity among the artistic and wealthy elite but, following *Histoire d'O,* numerous bourgeois couples also confessed to being enthusiasts. Most insisted that, far from threatening their relationships, it brought them closer together, as it had O and René.

Certain individuals from the subculture were suggested as models for O, including glamorous painter and sensualist Léonor Fini, who designed an owl's head mask similar to that worn by O at the ball. Aury later acknowledged her debt to Fini for this detail, and Fini produced a series of lithographs for a luxury edition of the book in which the mask features, but the affinity probably goes no further.

Even more gossip was excited by the identity of Réage, for which there were many candidates. Desclos even attended a dinner party where the hostess confided to her guests, "Henri has been *so* busy since he wrote *Histoire d'O*." The husband acted embarrassed, shushing his wife and swearing the guests to silence. Desclos looked down at her plate and said nothing.

A leading contender was young novelist and editor Alain Robbe-Grillet, whose affectless characters and impatience with traditional narrative resonated with the Réage book. He did nothing to discourage the rumors and even confessed his enthusiasm for sadomasochism. On a visit to Turkey in 1951, he had met Catherine Rstakian, a writer, actress and photographer who became his mistress and, later, wife. She cooperated in realizing his fantasies. Theirs was, she explained, "a sexual and emotional relationship which has fulfilled them both but would not suit everyone." She refused to apologize for their lifestyle and her role as a "submissive." Some of her pronouncements echoed those of *O*. "I want to be a 'woman-subject'," she said, "mistress of the game, enjoying the delaying of satisfaction, the preambles, the ornamentation of desire, the displacement of the sexual. A slap is a slap, a whiplash is a whiplash and they can hurt a lot [. . .] but these practices are framed, presented as a form of drama."

Rstakian also wrote her own erotic novel, *L'Image,* about two jaded sensualists who induct a beautiful innocent into their games. The book encouraged as much speculation as *Histoire d'O.* Was the woman based on Rstakian? If so, who was their young slave? Might Rstakian even be Pauline Réage? Robbe-Grillet ingeniously manipulated the gossip. He wrote a favorable introduction to *L'Image,* and, reasoning that the writer of *Histoire d'O* would not break incognito over so trifling a matter, signed it "Pauline Réage"— but lost his nerve before publication, abbreviating the signature to "P.R." He also coached Rstakian in how to sell herself. Disguised in heavy veils and using the pseudonym "Jean de Berg," she appeared on television, hinting broadly that she was Réage.

These intrigues aroused the suspicions of publisher Jérôme Lindon, Robbe-Grillet's boss at Les Éditions de Minuit. A colleague experimenting with computer technology offered to establish authorship definitively by running both texts through a program that analyzed style and word use. Shortly after, he reported to Lindon, as well as a nonplussed Robbe-Grillet and Rstakian, which, according to the computer, the same person not only wrote both the introduction and *Histoire d'O* but *L'Image* too.

Pauvert produced numerous printings of *Histoire d'O,* as well as selling the American rights to Grove Press, for whom Richard Seaver, as "Sabine d'Estrée," made an English translation. The book inspired luxury illustrated editions, as well as pastiches and parodies, and was adapted into a photo book and a graphic novel. A mediocre 1975 film version by Just Jaeckin, starring Corinne Clery, inaugurated some even less distinguished sequels.

Histoire d'O was to be Aury's only work of fiction. Aside from a small group of poems, *Songes (Dreams),* she confined her writing to reviews and translations. In 1969, Pauvert published *Retour à Roissy (Return to the Chateau).* Subtitled *Histoire d'O 2,* it comprised the chapter cut on Paulhan's advice and an essay, *Une Fille Amoureuse*

(A Girl in Love), in which, without revealing her identity, Desclos explained why she wrote the book. She completed it in the hospital room where Paulhan was dying, and where she slept every night for the four months preceding his death.

In 1963, Paulhan applied to become one of the only 40 members of the prestigious Academie Française. Unsure whether his involvement with *Histoire d'O* had impaired his reputation, he was alarmed, on entering the Academie chamber, to find that rivals had placed on each chair a copy of Pauvert's edition in its bright yellow cover. He was, however, elected decisively on the first ballot, signifying formally that *Histoire d'O* and the behavior it described had become part of the national culture.

~❖~

Footnote. Shortly before her death in 1998, Desclos confirmed her identity as Pauline Réage. An interviewer asked if she had ever been tempted to experience the torments of her heroine. She confessed that it held no appeal to her—although Paulhan, she said with a smile, would have been willing to inflict them. For herself, she was attracted to the idea of sex with many men at the same time—but, she sighed, in that case it was Paulhan who demurred.

Chapter 29.

THE CAROUSEL OF SEX: CATHERINE MILLET AND JACQUES HENRIC

The Sexual Life of Catherine M

No French spring is complete without its sexual page-turner. It generally depicts an attractive but reserved young woman submitting to the perverse whims of one or more bedroom athletes, often deliciously lower class. The true topic of such books is power—something which fascinates the French more than sex.

Histoire d'O was a precursor of this trend. A decade later, in *Emmanuelle,* Emmanuelle Arsan, former wife of a French diplomat in Thailand, would describe how she staved off boredom during his posting there by indulging in erotic adventures with partners of both sexes. (She subsequently confessed that her husband wrote the whole thing.) Michel Houellebecq followed in 1998 with *Les Particles Élémentaires (The Elementary Particles)* and in 2002 with *Platforme (Platform),* both about couples pursuing diminishing satisfaction via *échangiste* clubs and sexual tourism.

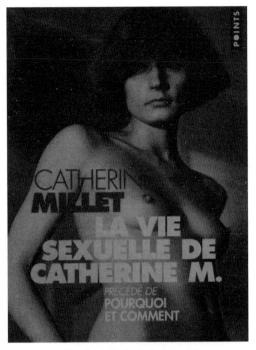

The Sexual Life of Catherine M

La Vie Sexuelle de Catherine M (The Sexual Life of Catherine M) a memoir by Catherine Millet, was the first winner of the new millennium. It detailed her thirty-year experience as a *partousier.* Her husband, Jacques Henric, followed with *Legendes de Catherine M (Legends of Catherine M),* documenting photographically her pleasure at exposing herself naked in public.

Neither book would have attracted much attention had the authors driven buses for a living, but both Henric and Millet belonged to the cultural elite, he as a novelist, she as editor of the monthly *Art Press,* author of the definitive history of French contemporary art and a regular guest on the intellectual TV discussion programs. Henric's œuvre included seven novels, all inspired by her. "A free woman, without guilt, is a beautiful gift for a novelist," he said.

La Vie Sexuelle didn't fit the Sadeian pattern of a heroine degraded or otherwise misused. Millet declined to play a modern O or updated Emmanuelle, nor did she belong in the bleak future proposed by Houellebecq. Nobody forced her to engage in her sexual adventures and she never experienced the tortures of Réage's heroine. As for her fellow *partousiers*, they were, unlike Houellebecq's characters, uniformly cheerful, gentle and kind. "The belief that sexuality is the most widely shared thing in the world comforts me in the thought that nothing bad would happen," she said as she embarked on a new encounter.

Millet wasn't particularly attractive, but possessed that sulky sexuality the French call *chienne*—bitchy. Even in her husband's photographs, however, she was expressionless. To those who labeled her book "joyless," Millet responded that sex should no more be a cause for levity than, say, Picasso's *Les Demoiselles d'Avignon*. Something so important, she argued, deserved to be experienced with discrimination and respect.

La partouze entered her life when she was 18. With three men and another young woman, she explored some of its permutations beside a secluded swimming pool near Lyon. She enjoyed the feeling of being used, comparing it to the excitement of a carnival ride. "I rushed into the tunnel of the ghost train, blindly, for the pleasure of being tossed around and seized at random. Or, if you like, swallowed, as is a frog by a snake." Of the numerous men and, occasionally, women with whom she shared her body over the next 30 years, about 50 left a lasting impression. The rest were a *montage* of faceless hands, lips, and genitals. Anonymity fed her pleasure. Naked on a table under bright lights, being caressed by a dozen hands, she visualized her body as the surface of a casino table, available for the entertainment of anybody who cared to play.

It was an open secret that, if, on any weekend night, you drove
to Porte Dauphine, an anonymous roundabout on the main route
west out of Paris, put on your turn indicator and began circling in
the slow lane, other cars would link up until the leader peeled off,
leading the group to some convenient location for a *partouze*. But
Millet dismissed "the carousel of Porte Dauphine" as middle-
class. She preferred private clubs, luxury apartments, country *cha-
teaux*—or, at the opposite end of the spectrum, parking stations,
workmens' huts and the Bois de Boulogne, the wooded park long
a popular hang-out of prostitutes, voyeurs and exhibitionists.

Some encounters were opportunistic. She had sex with her den-
tist and his nurse in the chair, and with moving men in their van
as they shifted paintings from airport to gallery, the driver watching in the rearview mirror. Aside from disguising their identities,
Millet's book omitted no detail of the people, their activities or its
rituals. Describing one *soirée* in a walled garden, she wrote, "Eric
installed me on one of the beds or couches placed in one of the
alcoves, and, following the etiquette of these events, took the ini-
tiative in undressing and exposing me. He would start to caress
and kiss me, and the relay was immediately taken up by others."

Millet met Jacques Henric in the early 1970s. They moved in
together, but only married in the 1990s—"for the taxes," she explained. Their lifestyle, classically self-absorbed, left little room
for such distractions as children. Instead, Henric, not a *partousier* himself, catered to his wife's desires, in particular her pleasure
in exposing herself publicly. *Legendes de Catherine M* documented
some of their excursions—to the railway station at Port-Bou, for
instance, on the French-Spanish border.

"Saturday 14th August 1999," wrote Henric in breathless cine-
matic shorthand. "*Le Talgo* heading for Barcelona passes through
at high speed. Catherine is seated on a bench. The wind from the
Talgo lifts the right panel of her dress. Her thigh is naked . . ."

More than the thigh, in fact—made abundantly clear as she stood and walked towards him, dress unbuttoned from neck to hem, but otherwise nude. One can imagine startled passengers staring out the window and thinking *I could swear I saw . . .*

Henric claimed the highest artistic aims for his photos. References to painters, authors and philosophers peppered his text. On the page showing Catherine, dress open, posed in a sunlit town square, he cited Lacan, Céline, Gombrowicz, Artaud, John Donne, Tina Modotti, Edward Weston, Aristotle and Buddha.

Port-Bou didn't attract Millet simply as one of the busiest stations in Europe. German theorist Walter Benjamin, author of the influential *The Work of Art in the Age of Mechanical Reproduction,* committed suicide there with his mistress in 1940 while fleeing from the Nazis. Henric described finding the hotel room where the couple spent their last night, then photographing Millet semi-naked in the cemetery where Benjamin is buried.

In the wake of her book, Millet continued to attract controversy. Interviewed by the press, she expressed regret at never having experienced rape, since it would have given her a better insight into its effects. She also spoke up for men who indulged in *frottage* in the Metro, rubbing up against women. "I have a certain compassion for the *frotteurs.* Someone who is reduced to that to find sexual satisfaction must be in misery."

About her activities, she was unapologetic. "I reveled in it. It's what I was truly good at. I loved particularly the anonymity, the abandonment, the sensation that one was glorying in this unbelievable freedom, this transcendence. I look back on it with nothing but pleasure. It was very important to me, to my identity, my ego, but it wasn't an addiction. I was never a nymphomaniac. I did not pounce on everything that moved. I never provoked. I made myself available. I enjoyed myself."

If the ideal life is one free of any need other than to experience pleasure and share it with others, without envy, jealousy or prejudice, her memoir came close to being a love story, but with no love object, only the pursuit of pure transcendence: an ideal the medieval troubadors and religious mystics understood.

~❖~

Footnote. Millet decided to write her memoir after learning that Henric, on whose approval and support she relied, had also enjoyed a number of affairs. In a later book, *Jealousy,* she described her attempts to reconcile her anguish over his infidelity with her own insistence on complete sexual freedom. What she had embraced in theory, she could not endure in practice.

Chapter 30.

CRAZY LOVE: LOVA MOOR AND ALAIN BERNARDIN

In the 1965 film *What's New Pussycat?*, Woody Allen, playing a writer in Paris, tells his friend Peter O'Toole that he's found work at the Crazy Horse nude cabaret.

"I help the girls dress and undress," he explains. "It's twenty francs a week."

"Not much," sympathizes O'Toole.

Allen shrugs. "It's all I can afford."

Woody didn't need to spell out the delights of such a job. With each decade, the reputation of "Le Crazy" for stylish sexuality has only improved.

When the French fall in love with America, they do so without reservation. Rocker Johnny Hallyday out-Elvised Elvis, Jean-Paul Belmondo made Humphrey Bogart look almost effeminate, and, compared to French hamburgers, the Big Mac was a cocktail nibble. No surprise, then, that when painter and art-dealer Alain Bernardin decided to exploit the cowboy mystique and introduce

France to square dancing, he did so in the very heart of the most prestigious part of Paris, just off the Champs-Élysées, in a "golden triangle" of Michelin-starred restaurants and five-star hotels. The 12 wine cellars he leased on rue Francois 1st for the club were even said to be on the site where Joséphine de Beauharnais danced *deshabilée* for Paul Barras before becoming the consort of Napoléon Bonaparte.

Friends such as the singer Bing Crosby and humorist Art Buchwald advised against the plan, particularly in the depths of a post-World War II slump, but Bernardin was adamant. Decorating the cellars in frontier style, he dressed his staff in jeans, Stetsons and lumberjack shirts, and found a French-speaking caller ready to teach Parisians how to Allemande Left and Do-Si-Do. The club took the name of the Crazy Horse Saloon after the Lakota chief who helped defeat Custer at the Little Bighorn.

From its 1951 opening, however, the Crazy Horse never made money, and Bernardin was ready to close it down when, in 1953, he saw a film about Minsky's famous New York burlesque theatre, and decided to adapt its recipe of high-style titillation to France. A raked auditorium replaced the dance floor, lighting became subdued, two doormen in Canadian Mounted Police uniforms vetted the clientele for drunkenness and inappropriate dress, and the Crazy Horse Saloon reopened as an erotic cabaret. In an inspired coup, Bernardin hired as his first headliner Micheline Bernardini, the Casino de Paris showgirl who had been the only woman courageous enough to model the just-invented Bikini swimsuit.

The upscale location that worked against it as a square dancing club gave the new Crazy Horse a piquant snob appeal. Concierges at the best hotels, their palms liberally greased, were happy to arrange a booking for their more adventurous guests, and Fouquet's, one of the most famous Champs-Élysées restaurants, began offering post-Crazy suppers.

Small, balding, fatherly, with grown children, Bernardin didn't fit the stereotype of the strip-club owner, which undoubtedly helped him succeed. From the start, he envisaged a show so discreet that the president of the republic could watch it without squirming or compromising his reputation—and where, moreover, he could return the next week with his wife.

No girls strutted on the bar and stuffed bills into their G-strings. Instead, spectators sat in darkness on red velvet couches, sipping champagne and watching a show so elaborate in its use of tinted and patterned lights that one could barely tell if the dancers were naked or not. There was little actual stripping. Instead, singly or in groups, wearing a few grams of summer-weight thistledown, dancers prowled the stage, or simply stood motionless, glowering into the darkness. The effect on audiences ranged from hypnosis to frenzy. One spectator, accustomed to American strip bars, so far forgot himself as to yell, "Get 'em off!" He was shushed by disapproving neighbors. "It was like we were listening to one of Beethoven's late quartets," he said indignantly.

"Bernardin was involved with every detail," recalled one dancer. "He created the concept of the show. He created its famous lighting. He chose the music, even wrote some lyrics. He drew sketches for costumes. He designed the theater. He didn't choreograph the numbers, but since he was a painter, he saw each dance number as if it were a painting. Therefore he had the whole thing in his head, and communicated that vision to the choreographers."

Alain Bernardin and Lava Moor

Shrewdly, Bernardin showcased the work of fashion-designer friends such as Paco Rabanne, whose gowns of linked plastic and metal discs suited the Crazy Horse style. When Salvador Dalí saw the show and returned to sketch rehearsals, Bernardin added a sequence in which a dancer slithered over and around the famous red velvet couch designed by Dalí in the shape of Mae West's lips.

Conventional strippers traditionally took such pseudonyms as Stormy Tempest or, more subtly, Cha Landres (pronounced "Shall Undress") but Bernardin elevated the practice into realms of caricature, christening his girls Akky Masterpiece, Tiny Semaphore, Paula Flashback, Queeny Blackpool, Zia Paparazzi, Volga Moskovskaya, even Fuzzy Logic. The names implied that they came from all over the world, but while the troupe always included a few Britons, Canadians and the occasional Australian, Bernardin's taste for compact blondes with wide, feral smiles, medium breasts and generous bottoms meant that Eastern Europe predominated.

Choreographer George Balanchine regularly visited le Crazy, and the show so fascinated Toni Bentley, for ten years his star dancer at the New York City Ballet, that she asked Bernardin for a job. He turned her down, not for any lack of talent but because her measurements didn't conform to his rule that all dancers be between 5-feet, 5-inches and 5-feet, 6-inches tall and identically proportioned. Their physical features, from eyes to crotch, had to line up precisely. He did allow Bentley backstage, where she collected some make-up secrets. Dior No. 004 powder blush gave the girls' skin a uniform creamy pallor, while they owed their pubic triangles, like the moustaches of Charlie Chaplin and Groucho Marx, to Leichner Black greasepaint.

Rock star Prince was one of many celebrities who angled for a "private meeting" with the troupe but was indignantly turned down by Bernardin. "We were his girls," said one, "almost like his daughters. He was very possessive of us." His rules would not have been out of place in a Swiss finishing school. "We had a private exit so no one would see us leaving without our make-up on," said one dancer. "He didn't allow us to meet men or date anyone who worked there. He didn't allow us to talk to stagehands. Our boyfriends could not pick us up in front of the building—always around the block."

The Crazy Horse became the acceptable face of French eroticism, imitated around the world: Bernardin even fought a landmark court case over the pirating of the name by a Las Vegas show, only to later license it there and in many other territories. When Abbé Pierre, France's Mother Teresa, pleaded for help to feed the homeless during the bitter winter of 1974, Bernardin put the premises and cast at his disposal to raise funds. Such gestures made it permissible, even fashionable, to be seen there. John Kennedy attended while still a senator. Liza Minnelli, Elvis Presley and Prince Albert of Monaco came. So did Madonna—three times. Bernardin held up the show for almost an hour when Sammy Davis Jr. announced he was on his way, and Jimmy Connors consoled himself there after losing the French Open.

In 1975, Bernardin auditioned an imperious young blonde from La Grève-sur-Mignon in the southern region of Charente-Maritime. Marie-Claude Jourdain told him she'd been dancing naked from infancy. "My parents made me get up on the kitchen table when I had taken my bath," she said. "I heard 'What a pretty body this little girl has,' so I would come down the stairs naked and wait for my father and my mother to ask me. I liked it."

The pseudonym Bernardin assigned her, Lova Moor, proved prescient, since, repeating the fable of Pygmalion and Galatea, he fell in love with his creation. After two years during which she became leader of the troupe, he tried to launch her as an actress. In 1977, the girls went "on holiday" to the Cannes Film Festival, where they were photographed cavorting on the beach with

Arnold Schwarzenegger. Seeing them inspired Italian producers to hire the entire company for the comedy *Week-end à l'Italienne*. Bernardin pushed his protegée in front of the camera, hoping she would shine. Instead, she was humiliatingly eclipsed.

Despite the 30-year difference in their ages, Bernardin and Jourdain married in 1985. May/September marriages are a cliché of show business, often mocked, even by those involved, and this one followed an all too familiar pattern. Jourdain's interest in both the Crazy Horse and Bernardin waned after the first few years. Undeterred by her failure on screen, she tried singing, reaching the limit of her talent as a diminutive Valkyrie, pacing statuesquely around the stage, miming to forgettable Europop. As she found her level as a guest and occasional presenter of TV talk and variety shows, rumors circulated of an imminent separation. In September 1995, at the age of 78, Alain Bernardin was found dead in his office at the club, having shot himself in the head. One obituary offered a stanza from Voltaire as an appropriate epitaph. "One dies twice, I see that well./Unable to love or be loved –/That's unbearable./By comparison, death is nothing."

~ ❖ ~

Footnote. In 1966, the Crazy Horse inspired British theater critic Kenneth Tynan to produce a stage revue of erotic sketches scripted by John Lennon, Jules Feiffer, Edna O'Brien and Sam Shepard, among others. It played around the world to mixed reviews but satisfactory profits, and was widely copied. A devotee of spanking, Tynan took the title from a painting by Surrealist Clovis Trouille of the female buttocks, entitled *"Oh, quel cul t'a"*/What an ass you have! – or, phonetically, *Oh! Calcutta!*

Chapter 31.

PUTTIN'ON THE RITZ: DIANA, PRINCESS OF WALES, AND DODI AL-FAYED

In August 1997, Diana, Britain's former Princess of Wales, and her lover Dodi Al-Fayed, flew into Paris in his family's jet. The next day they visited a mansion on the edge of the Bois de Boulogne, once the home of the Duke of Windsor, who, as Edward VIII, abdicated in 1936 rather than give up his American mistress. Dodi's father, Mohamed Al-Fayed, owned the house and had commissioned its restoration but Dodi and his paramour didn't stay long, preferring a suite at the Hôtel Ritz, another possession of Al-Fayed *père*. Leaving the hotel that night, pursued by paparazzi, a chauffeur crashed their Mercedes in an underpass below the Pont d'Alma. Both Diana and Dodi died.

In an era of "fake news," it made sense that the romance of Diana and Dodi should have been a concoction. Diana cynically

Princes Diana and Dodi Memorial at Harrods, 2011

took up with Fayed to hit back at the family of her estranged husband, and to excite the jealousy of the lover who dumped her, Pakistani heart surgeon Hasnat Khan. She lured the world's press to the Al-Fayed family villa off the Mediterranean resort of St. Tropez, and, as boats bristling with telephoto lenses circled like sharks, romped in a succession of swimsuits with her two sons and Dodi. When her efforts had no immediate effect, she sent the boys back to England and, with Dodi, flew to Paris. There was an element of destiny in their visit to a house where another member of the British royal family had lived in exile. Equally, her death could not have had a more appropriate setting than the Ritz.

A fog of scandal enveloped the Ritz from the moment it was conceived in 1898 out of an alliance between Swiss hotelier César Ritz and French *chef de cuisine* Auguste Escoffier. Both worked for London's Savoy Hôtel at the time, and collaborated to loot it of equipment, supplies and staff for the Paris project. When the Savoy management, having uncovered their network of fake companies and kickbacks, dismissed the two men for "gross negligence and breaches of duty, and mismanagement," police had to be called to evict them and their knife-brandishing kitchen staff.

The new hotel's façade, formerly part of an 18th-century town house, as well as its location on Place Vendôme, surrounded by jewelers, fashion houses and luxury restaurants, and overshadowed by a column celebrating the victories of Napoléon I, reflected Ritz's plan to attract a more trendy clientele than the older and more reputable Crillon and Meurice. It was among the first hotels in Europe to furnish each room with an *en suite* bathroom, electricity, and a telephone, while Escoffier's flair for themed banquets and parties attracted show-business personalities and others for whom money was no object.

Staff became expert at accommodating idiosyncrasies. Reception raised not so much as an eyebrow at the "nieces," "wards," or "secretaries" with whom guests arrived. One could check in under a pseudonym and, if necessary, settle the bill in cash, while the cleaning staff knew to dispose discreetly of any items found tangled in the sheets. When, in the 1939 film *Midnight,* Francis Lederer asks penniless showgirl Claudette Colbert for the name of her hotel, she improvises: ("I'll give you three guesses." "The Ritz?" "Right first time.") Checking in at midnight with only the clothes she's wearing, she wakes next morning to find that, thanks to a wealthy "protector," the management has conjured up, overnight, a *haute couture* wardrobe and a limousine, with chauffeur.

For the rich and gifted of Paris, the Ritz became their canteen. From time to time, Marcel Proust sent his housekeeper or chauffeur to collect a late-night snack and a bottle of cold beer. As he often had these urges after the kitchen staff had gone home, the manager, Olivier Debascat, showed him where the beer and ice were kept, and even provided a key. Today's management has wrung the last drop of profit from the association by designating one room as the Proust Salon, advertised as "a small world in itself, an intimate place to take refuge in the cocoon of its woodwork to savor its voluptuous serenity." They stopped short, however, of putting cork on the walls.

"Ritz" and "ritzy" became synonymous with luxury. Irving Berlin wrote *Puttin' on the Ritz* to describe how one dressed to impress and Cole Porter added a verse to *Let's Do It:* "The world admits/Bears in pits do it/Even Pekingeses/At the Ritz do it." Since it wasn't copyrighted, many others pirated the name. It was attached to a brand of savory cracker, and American vaudeville performer Al Joachim, spotting it on a laundry van, adopted it for the family act, turning The Ritz Brothers into Hollywood headliners. The name features in Scott Fitzgerald's 1922 novella *A Diamond as Big as the Ritz,* but the events of the story take place far from the hotel. Fitzgerald spent almost no time there, and Ernest Hemingway describes in *A Moveable Feast* how its head barman asked, long after his death, "Who is this Mister Fitzgerald that people keep asking me about?"

"So we came to the Ritz hotel and the Ritz Hôtel was divine," wrote Anita Loos in her 1925 bestseller *Gentlemen Prefer Blondes,* about two American girls on the prowl in Paris. It pleases her heroine, Lorelei Lee, that "a girl can sit in a delightful bar and have delicious champagne cocktails and look at all the important French people in Paris." Loos omitted to mention that the Ritz bar excluded women, who were exiled to the Ladies' Bar, described in a 1927 guide book as "a tiny box-like room, barely 15 feet square, densely packed [with] American Flappers, Cinema Queens, stage belles and alimony spenders."

Couturier Gabrielle "Coco" Chanel helped bolster the hotel's reputation when she moved there in 1937, making it her home until her death in 1971. The proportions of Place Vendôme, as seen from her window, inspired the design of the *flaçon* for her most famous fragrance, Chanel No. 5. When the Germans occupied Paris in 1940, they declared the Ritz, on the flimsy pretext of César Ritz's Swiss citizenship, to be "neutral territory." *Reichsmarschall* Hermann Göring moved into its Imperial suite, a convenient place to meet the dealers who lined up to offer him looted treasures. Coco Chanel assured her continued safety and comfort by taking a German lover. She'd known the handsome young part-British Baron Hans Gunther von Dincklage before the war but he became even more attractive to her when Hitler tasked him with adapting the lucrative French fabric and fashion industries to post-war use by the Reich.

Chanel shut down her headquarters on nearby rue Cambon and laid off 4,000 employees, but otherwise lived in the hotel much as she had done in peacetime. She came and went by the staff entrance and, when an air raid warning sounded, descended into the cellars, preceded by a hotel employee carrying her gas mask on a satin pillow. As news spread of the Ritz's relaxed policy towards the occupying power, the actress Arletty and her German lover Hans Jürgen Soehring also moved in. Arletty articulated the philosophy of women like Chanel and herself when she explained to those who condemned her behavior "My heart is French—but my ass is international."

Von Dincklage recruited Chanel as an agent of German intelligence, code name "Westminster," convincing his superiors her contacts in British high society might be useful in back-door negotiations. With his help, she attempted to claw back the rights to the perfume business she had sold to a Jewish company. She fled to Switzerland as the Allies approached Paris in 1944, not returning until her prewar friend Winston Churchill had her record as a collaborator expunged.

How did two such unlikely people as Princess Diana and Dodi Fayed ever become involved? The answer lies in the history of Dodi's father, Mohamed Al-Fayed, and his attempts to be accepted as an English gentleman by a culture that, however much it needed their money, detested such self-made citizens of their lost empire.

In 1986, when Diana was still married to Charles, Al-Fayed attended a polo match at Windsor in which the Prince of Wales was playing. Already owner of the Ritz and London's premier department store, Harrods, possessor of the coveted warrant to supply goods to the Royal Family, Al-Fayed was eager for acceptance by the palace. He even hired the Duke of Windsor's former valet to coach him in the behavior required of a courtier. As a generous benefactor of the organization staging the polo match, Mohamed expected to be seated next to the Queen. She, however, preferred the company of her horsey friends, and delegated the task to the family's least exalted member, Diana.

The two outsiders found they had much in common but it was another decade before Diana met Al-Fayed's glamorous playboy son, at the premiere of Steven Spielberg's film *Hook,* in which Dodi was an investor. Shunned and spurned by her husband and his relatives, she was ripe to be seduced, not only by Dodi's exotic foreign charm, but by his lifestyle of private planes, luxurious yachts and French Riviera estates. Mohamed, already an admirer of the princess who befriended him and contemptuous of the models and other glitzy riffraff with whom his son shared his life, gave his blessing to the relationship, issuing invitations that could only encourage a romance.

Such an invitation brought Diana and Dodi to their fatal meeting at the Ritz. In the summer of 1996, Mohamed invited Diana, devastated by the breakup with Charles, to holiday with her sons William and Harry on his yacht, the *Jonikal,* moored at Saint-Tropez. Acquired a few days earlier for $30 million, the *Jonikal* offered Diana the luxury absent from her chilly home among the Windsors, while the Al-Fayeds lavished on her the affection and respect her in-laws always withheld. Diana succumbed, and her appointment with death under the Pont d'Alma became just a matter of time.

~ ❖ ~

Footnote. After France recriminalized prostitution in 1946, some *poules de luxe* set up shop in hotel cocktail lounges. Once the Ritz belatedly lifted its ban on women, they colonized its main bar, joined by enterprising schoolgirls from the better *lycees.* Known as *sucettes* (lollipops), they pedaled there after class in their white knee socks and short plaid skirts, chained their bikes to the railings outside, took a seat in the bar and waited for some gentleman to buy them an *eau à la menthe* and invite them up to his room.

Chapter 32.

ENTRANCED: JOHN BAXTER AND MARIE-DOMINIQUE MONTEL

I never expected to figure in a love story, let alone a Paris tale. Such things happened in books, not to those who write them. Nor did it seem like a love story while it took place—which is probably true of the accounts that fill this book. Love has no "story": it's only later, in hindsight, that the narrative emerges, frequently burnished by nostalgia.

In a semitropical city like Sydney, Australia, the fall is sometimes distinguished by a monsoon-like series of downpours that daily inundate the city in ceaseless and torrential rain. The fall of 1987 was such a season. It resonated with my state of mind. My second marriage had just ended in divorce, and a friend arriving from Los Angeles found me sitting alone in an empty house, undecided on the direction my life should now take.

John Baxter and Marie Dominique with daughter
Louise at their wedding

Sally—I'll use fictional names for obvious reasons—was a movie
executive whose brother, a screenwriter, had come to Australia a
few months before and not been heard from since. (We learned he
only stayed a few days and, as depressed as I was by the weather,
went on to Fiji.)

She and I hung out for a while, but I was poor company.

"You're wasting your time here," she said. "Why not come to
California? I'm sure we can find something for you to do."

As my ex-wife was American, I had a green card, and there was,
I had to agree, little to keep me in this sodden corner of the world.
Within what, in memory, seemed only a few days, though was actually a couple of months, I was unpacking my bags in the apartment on Veteran Avenue in the Los Angeles suburb of Westwood
that would be my home for the next two years.

The contrast with Sydney could not have been greater. As widely
advertised, the sun shone all the time in California. The one occasion on which a small shower slipped through, Sally intercepted
a few drops, licked her fingers and said "Orange juice." Just ten
minutes' drive away was the beach at Santa Monica. True, nobody

swam in its polluted waters—a popular t-shirt carried the image of a flounder's skeleton, glowing green—but from the terrace of a café, viewed over one of those gargantuan American breakfasts, the Pacific looked as pure as in any Esther Williams musical.

At one such meal, Sally asked, "I wonder if you could do something for me. Well, more for a friend, really."

The friend—call her Sasha—was another movie executive, though a few rungs above Sally's level. Her lover had just died, and she'd taken his loss hard; so hard that she even spoke of suicide. What she needed, Sally suggested, was someone with whom to hang out; to show around town, explain things—to distract her from her troubles.

To be honest, I didn't find the prospect very inviting. To turn up at someone's apartment and find her with her head in the gas oven . . .

"I'm sure it won't come to that," Sally said. Seeing I wasn't reassured, she went on "You like science fiction films. Did you see . . . ?" And named a title counted among the best such movies ever made.

"Of course! It's a masterpiece. I love it."

"Well, she was the producer. And the boyfriend who died was X," she said, naming a famous and recently deceased director. I wasn't particularly a fan of X's blood-boltered action, distinguished by a gleeful excess of slaughter, but of his eminence there was no doubt. For me not to step up in this situation began to look like a betrayal of everything expected of a cinéphile.

As it turned out, keeping company with Sasha was no chore. She charmed me as readily as she had X—who, I soon came to believe, had not deserved her.

"Sally says he used to beat you up," I said.

"No!" she replied. "Oh, well, yes, sometimes . . . a little bit. But it was the cocaine. It made him crazy."

"And how about all these other women he screwed?"

"There weren't *that* many. And he always came back to me."

Clearly X had taken up residence in a corner of her brain and would not easily be dislodged.

From time to time, the question of suicide came up. It soon became clear she didn't find it attractive as a surcease from the pain of loss so much as in the naïve belief that she and X might find one another again after death.

"Well, that's always possible . . . I guess," I said skeptically.

"Not for me," she said. "I'm Jewish. We don't believe in Heaven and the Pearly Gates and all that *mishegoss*." She paused reflectively. "Of course, I could always convert."

"Convert to what?"

"Well, to a religion that *does* believe in . . . " A gesture encompassed all the promises of paradise.

While I had been brought up a Catholic and briefly considered entering the priesthood, this was uncharted territory. Wasn't there a question of . . . well, *belief*? I could see Sasha's attempt at conversion mirroring that of Rex Mottram in Evelyn Waugh's *Brideshead Revisited*. The priest instructing him laments that Rex will accept anything if it will smooth the way to marrying Julia Flyte. "Yesterday I asked him whether Our Lord had more than one nature. He said 'Just as many as you say, Father.' Then again I asked him 'Supposing the Pope looked up and saw a cloud and said, "It's going to rain," would that be bound to happen?' 'Oh, yes, Father.' 'But supposing it didn't?' He thought a moment and said, 'I suppose it would be sort of raining spiritually, only we were too sinful to see it.'"

But humoring her seemed a wiser move than scorn, so for a few weeks we crisscrossed the city auditioning belief systems—not a difficult task since, as Frank Lloyd Wright remarked, "Tip the world over on its side and everything loose will land in Los Angeles."

I'd had a taste of what to expect when Ken Russell, while directing *Crimes of Passion* there in 1984, decided to marry his girlfriend, and suggested that Tony Perkins, who played a demented divine in the film, should perform the ceremony. It concerned Perkins that he wasn't a real priest but he found a sect that, for a modest fee, would ordain him on the spot. Thus empowered, he tied the entirely legal knot in the chapel of the old liner *Queen Mary,* transformed into a hotel and permanently moored at Long Beach.

Sasha and I talked about Catholicism first, since it was the creed I knew best. Though no longer a believer, I retained an affection for its liturgy and ritual. Adapted, altered and dumbed down over the centuries, it resembled a once-grand stately home, riddled with boarded-up attics, staircases ending in blank walls, and closets filled with moldering vestments and implements of obscure but ominous function. Surely some sleepy side chapel, smelling of incense, dust and beeswax, could offer a refuge to Sasha and her dead demon lover.

But too many weeks spent on Mexican locations with X in the back streets of Durango and Sonora had left her with a different and indelible vision of the Holy Roman Church, a Goya-esque frieze of torturers in cardinal's purple and black-clad crones mumbling over their rosaries or painfully inching on their knees across bare stone floors towards that anguished figure on the cross.

After that, we moved briskly through the standard protestant offshoots, going on to spend time with Buddhists, a tarot card reader, a lady who actually used a somewhat yellowed crystal ball, and a housewifey medium who sat at a card table on stage in a church hall in the suburb of Encino, clutching the hand of her husband as she claimed to channel the spirit of 1920s faith healer Edgar Cayce. Following an hour of rambling for which the medium assumed Cayce's real-life croaking voice, reminiscent of the demonically possessed Linda Blair in *The Exorcist,* Sasha stood up.

"Fuck this," she said. "Let's eat. Do you fancy Chinese?"

I thought this debacle had ended her search but a few days later she rang and asked without preamble, "Have you ever been hypnotized?"

"No," I said cautiously. "Why?"

She explained that, according to the *Los Angeles Times,* a man using hypnotism in a religious context had achieved some remarkable results. At first glance, there appeared no obvious way in which the two could be connected, but the range and variety of Californian eccentricity made me cautious.

"Well, why not try it?" I said. "It can't hurt." Considering some of the people we'd visited, the idea seemed almost conventional.

"No fear!" she replied. "*You* try it. And if it's kosher, I *might.*"

The following Saturday found me driving through the outskirts of City of Commerce, one of the city's more seedy suburbs, a wilderness of used car lots and 24/7 poker parlors. The home of Saul, the investigator, a tiny box of an apartment in a hive of such places, was consistent with the neighborhood. It featured a vinyl shag carpet of indeterminate shade, comprehensively and ominously stained, and a popcorn ceiling from which dangled a macramé potholder holding the decayed remains of an *aspidistra elatior* or Mother-in-law's Tongue.

Saul himself, however, was entirely legitimate and obviously sincere. He had a degree in psychology and worked in a large mental hospital, where he routinely employed hypnotism in treating the mentally ill. Like André Breton and the Surrealists, he had noticed significant links between their behavior and the unconscious, and set out to explore them.

"But what exactly do you hope to achieve?" I asked.

"Well, basically," he said, with a "Here goes" expression, "we're looking for people who knew Jesus Christ."

I blinked. "You mean 'born again' Christians? Because I must tell you right off, I'm not one. When it comes to belief, I hover somewhere between agnostic and atheist."

"No, nothing like that," he said.

Light dawned. "You don't mean *reincarnated?*"

The west and the western United States in particular was going through one of its periodic flirtations with eastern religion, and specifically the concept of transmigration of souls. Actress Shirley MacLaine was its most insistent shill. Her claims to have lived as a Buddhist monk, a Mongol nomad, an Inca child and a Roman soldier, not to mention having existed a million years ago in Atlantis, made her the darling of the talk shows and launched a vogue for "past life regressions." Soon, every cab driver or dry cleaner in Hollywood claimed to have been someone far more interesting in their past. Napoléons and Cleopatras lurked in coffee shops, eager to recount their memories of Waterloo or Marc Antony, and Come-As-You-Were parties encouraged guests to arrive in costumes consistent with their previous lives.

I tried not to be too vehement in my dismissal of Saul's apparently sincere belief. In response, he was politely defensive.

"A lot of people feel that way," he conceded, "but we've achieved some remarkable results. And since you've come all this way . . . "

It was a persuasive argument, partly because it would avoid the need to tell Sasha that I'd driven out there for nothing. On the other hand, the presence nearby of a large secondhand bookshop called The Book Baron presented a tempting alternative way to spend the afternoon. What if I had let the bibliophile in me make the choice? How different my life would have been. Or might the Jungians be right and, no matter how I acted, the cosmic mechanism would have delivered me exactly where I ended up?

As so often happened, the decision went to inertia. I'd come this far, as Saul said, and I had to admit to a certain curiosity.

"OK," I said. "Let's do it. What happens next?"

If you have ever been hypnotized, you will know the answer: an invitation to lie down, in this case on Saul's distressed sofa, upholstered in nap-worn brown corduroy; the suggestion to fix my eyes on some object—I chose the hook of that sad plant holder—and to count backwards from one hundred until I felt the need to stop counting, and close my eyes, which in my case came in the upper seventies.

I'd elected to remember what happened while in a trance, so what I experienced was a sense of ease similar to that which preceded drifting into sleep. Part of me knew I could open my eyes at any time—if I wished. But there was just no reason to do so at the moment. And in this state I found it easy to recall events when Saul asked, from somewhere out of sight behind me, to remember where I was at 10 years old, and what I was doing . . .

It continued like that for an indeterminate time, which I later found to be almost three hours, but ended when, in my memory of life before the age of 4 or 5, there was only darkness. It seemed I had never lived before; never met Julius Caesar or Alexander the Great, never shared a lunch with Shirley MacLaine in Atlantis, least of all remembered, as did Salvador Dalí, the moment my father's sperm fertilized my mother's egg.

"I'm sorry," I said, when Saul released me from the trance. "I wasn't much use."

"It happens," he said. Consolingly, he added, "Perhaps yours is a young soul. It's only just begun its voyage towards enlightenment."

We chatted over a cup of watery decaf. After a while, he brought out what he clearly regarded as the crown jewel of his research; some dozens of pages, closely written, in which one of his subjects described how, between incarnations, she had spent some time in paradise.

It seemed that inhabitants of heaven slept communally in airy, spacious rooms, then woke to spend the day sitting on benches in green fields, absorbing the wisdom of the Elders.

I wanted to say, "This isn't heaven. It's *college*," but stifled the impulse.

"I'm really sorry," I said, handing it back. "Not coming up with anything at all."

"It's not important," he said. "But I appreciate your time. And I'd like to give you a gift."

I tried not to look around at his apartment, the reflection of an obviously frugal life, but he caught my inclination.

"I didn't mean money," he said. "I mean a post-hypnotic gift. If you agree, I'll put you back into a trance. Then I'll ask you to name the three things that have given you greatest pleasure in life. As you name each one, I'll squeeze your left wrist—and in the future, every time you squeeze that wrist, you will re-experience some of that pleasure."

This didn't seem stranger than other things I'd be asked to do since I came to Hollywood, and I was curious to see if my choices would differ under hypnosis.

The first suggested they would not, since it was simply the pleasure of sitting down each morning at my computer and addressing the blank page. I would have responded very much like that even without hypnosis.

Saul squeezed my wrist and said, "So what's the second?"

This was where things diverged from what I anticipated—since I began to weep. Tears flooded down my cheeks—in itself an unexpected feeling—and I heard myself repeating, "Who would have thought it would be a song?"

The song was *Finishing the Hat* by Stephen Sondheim. His work and its themes of loneliness, isolation, a lack of understanding and communication between even intimates had moved me ever since I saw a production of *Company* in Sydney. The song that made me weep came from his 1986 show *Sunday In the Park With George*. The Sunday in question occurs in the summer of 1884, the park is situated on an island in the Seine called La Grande Jatte, a popular spot to promenade or swim, and the "George" with whom we share the afternoon is the painter Georges Seurat, who has gone there to make sketches for a canvas. His mistress accompanies him but he becomes so involved in his work that another man lures her away. Her absence, when he notices it, depresses Seurat, but he consoles himself with the satisfaction of having created something more enduring than love: a hat, where there never was a hat.

Obviously the song resonated with my present marital state, which affected me more than I admitted, even to myself. In releasing me from those inhibitions, Saul had allowed some long-suppressed tears to flow.

Once again, he squeezed my wrist, "Well, let's have the third," he said.

And the roof fell in. Or, rather, it disappeared, and I was in a different place at a different time.

It was the open air, and winter, and no longer Los Angeles, or even America. Cold seeped through the soles of my shoes and wind bit at my ears. I was eating *pommes frites* dabbed with sharp French mustard, sharing them from a cone of paper with the girl on my arm. I didn't need to see her face to know she was my lover of the time, and we were just emerging from the *marché aux puces* at Clignancourt, on the northern edge of Paris.

I knew it was Paris and also that the date was November 2, 1979, just as I knew that, in a moment, we would encounter a crowd standing silent and three deep along the sidewalk. Out in the street, police would be milling around a BMW painted in the sepulchral silvery-grey known as Anthrazitgrau, its doors wide open, radio tinnily playing a number by The Clash, windscreen punctured by twenty bullet holes. Less than an hour earlier, the gangster Jacques Mesrine had occupied one seat and his girlfriend Sylvia Jeanjacquot the other. He was now dead, she badly injured after the police ambush that terminated the life and career of France's Public Enemy Number One.

As quickly as it took to describe, the vision disappeared, leaving only a sense of cold, a taste of grease and salt, the hint of Guerlain perfume and a glimpse of a fox fur coat collar rippling in the wind.

"What was *that?*" I gasped.

"Tell me," Saul frowned. "I'm assuming it didn't have anything to do with Jesus Christ."

As he released me from the trance and squeezed my wrist, I described the experience as best I could. Part of me noted dispassionately how closely it tallied with the flashes of memory documented by Proust in *À la Recherche du Temps Perdu*. I would read him now with heightened comprehension.

"But I don't understand," I said. "Clignancourt . . . Mesrine . . . that was . . . " I did a quick calculation. "seven years ago. I haven't been back to Paris since. I haven't seen *her* since. I mean, we exchange Christmas cards, the occasional note, but otherwise . . . Why her? Why Paris."

"I've no idea," Saul said. "But Paris obviously means a great deal to you. Or is it only Paris?"

No, it wasn't only Paris. This was more than a particularly pointed stab of nostalgia. Rather, my memory had played a chord to which many notes contributed. Paris was one, perhaps the death of Mesrine another, but in their totality they added up to Her.

I drove back to Westwood in a daze and sat for hours staring at the television but not watching it. She had been a radio journalist then; presumably still was. I looked at my watch and did some mental arithmetic. It was 2 a.m. in Paris. I knew she got up early most days to read the morning news. Our relationship had been a succession of sleepy goodbyes and coffee-flavored kisses before I turned over and went back to sleep.

Six hours later, at midnight Los Angeles time, I rang her up.

We talked for more than an hour: fortunately, she had moved on from reading the morning news. Six weeks later, she flew into Los Angeles. Two weeks after that, I sold everything I owned and moved to Paris. I've been there, and married to her, ever since.

Maybe there really is such a thing as true love.

~ ❖ ~

Footnote. When Marie-Dominique became pregnant with our daughter Louise, we swapped her tiny studio on Place Dauphine for the more spacious apartment of my mother-in-law-to-be Claudine. Later, we bought it from her and have lived there ever since. It wasn't for some months, however, that I learned Sylvia Beach and Adrienne Monnier once made their home two floors below us, and every great figure of expatriate literature, at some time or other, mounted the same staircase up which I labored with a toddler on my shoulders.

And yes (since it's something almost everyone asks who hears this story), there is still the ghost of a tingle when I squeeze my left wrist.

Is there a lesson to be learned from all these stories? I can think of at least one—that, contrary to Scott Fitzgerald's gloomy dictum, there *are* second acts in most lives, American or otherwise, and that love is the key to their discovery.

Of my own experience, I think often of the final line from the Robert Bresson film *Pickpocket*, when Michel, the thief, is finally able to say to the woman who has rescued and redeemed him, "Oh, Jeanne, to reach you at last, what a strange path I had to take."

INDEX

M

ABOUT THE AUTHOR

John Baxter is an Australian-born writer, journalist, lecturer, translator, and screenwriter. He has called Paris home since 1989, after living in Sydney, London, Dublin and Los Angeles.

His writing career began in his teens while living in a small Australian country town. His science fiction stories appeared in British and American magazines, and he compiled the first anthology of Australian work in the genre. He also developed a love of the cinema, which impelled him to become a film critic and historian. After writing the first history of the Australian cinema in 1968, he moved to London, where he quickly established himself as an authority on film history. He lectured and wrote widely, broadcast on radio and television, served on the jury of European film festivals and spent two years as Visiting Professor at Hollins University in Virginia.

In 1989 he married the French filmmaker Marie Dominique Montel and relocated in Paris. A chance meeting with Féderico Fellini led to an invitation to write the biography of the legendary director, followed by similar studies of, among others, Steven Spielberg, George Lucas, Ken Russell, Stanley Kubrick, Woody Allen, Josef von Sternberg and Robert DeNiro.

He also began writing about his new home and its rich cultural history. His books on France include *Chronicles of Old Paris, The Golden Moments of Paris, The French Riviera and its Artists, Eating Eternity: Food, Art and Literature in France,* ("delightful" *New York Times*). Of John's work, the *Los Angeles Times* wrote "We are the beneficiaries of John Baxter's considerable, vivid love for the expatriate life in Paris," and the *Boston Globe* called "reading John Baxter the next best thing to a Paris vacation."

John is a keen cook, as well an authority on and collector of rare books, the theme of his award-winning memoir *A Pound of Paper: Confessions of a Book Addict.* He also leads literary walking tours of Paris. Details are available on his website, www.johnbaxterparis.com.

CREDITS

Page 3: Les Liaisons Dangereuses by Georges Barbier, 1920s, Collection of John Baxter; Page 6: Beauty and the Beast, 1946, ©DisCina; Page 10: Choosing girls in brothel, Collection of John Baxter; Page 14: The Merry Widow, 1934, ©MGM; Page 25: Josephine signing the act of her divorce by E.M. Ward, 1853, National Gallery of Victoria, Melbourne; Page 32: Drawing of George Sand by Alfred de Musset, 1833; Page 36: Rolla by Henri Gervex, 1878, Musée d'Orsay; Page 39: By the Table, Henri Fantin-Latour, 1872, Musée d'Orsay; Page 45: Suicide of General Boulanger at the cemetery of Ixelles, on the tomb of Marguerite, Petit Journal, October 10, 189; Page 50: Adèle Hugo, c. 1856; Page 56: Céleste Albaret; Page 62 and 63: Amedeo Modigliani and Jeanne Hébuterne (1898–1920) in Modigliani's studio rue de la Grande-Chaumière, at Montparnasse. c. 1918; Page 70: Colette, Willy and the dog Toby, c. 1905; Page 77: Gloria Swanson and husband, 1925, Library of Congress; Page 82: Jules et Jim (1962) poster, ©Les Films du Carrossem SEDIF; Page 91: Raymond Radiguet by Man Ray, 1922; Page 99: Jean Rhys, Ford Madox Ford and Stella Bowen; Page 102: Opium den in Paris, c. 1928, Collection of John Baxter; Page 109: Gala Diakonova and Salvador Dali, 1930s; Page 114 and 115: Elsa-Triolet, 1925 and Louis Aragon, c. 1929; Page 122: Le Violon d'Ingres by Man Ray, 1924; Page 133: President John F. Kennedy attends dinner for Minister of State for Cultural Affairs of France, André Malraux, 1962, John F. Kennedy Library and Museum; Page 138: The Early Diary of Anaïs Nin, Vol 4 (1927 – 1931), 1986; Page 147: Sylvia Beach and her partner Adrienne Monnier, 1928, Collection of John Baxter; Page 154: Pat Paterson and Charles Boyer, 1935; Page 160: Belgian artists at the home of Victor Servranckx (June 1922); from left to right: (top) René Magritte, E.L.T. Mesens, Victor Servranckx, Pierre-Louis Flouquet, Pierre Bourgeois; (bottom) Georgette Berger, Pierre Broodcoorens, Henriette Flouquet; Page 165: PARIS—1947, Singer Edith Piaf is surrounded by her friends, including middleweight boxing champion Marcel Cerdan, whom she was having an affair with, sings one of her many successes at a café table in Paris circa 1947; Page 170: Jean-Paul Sartre and Simone de Beauvoir playing at a fairground on one of their first dates (1929); Page 177: Ernest Hemingway sits with his fourth wife Mary in Cuba. 1948, John F. Kennedy Library and Museum; Page 185: Juliette Greco and Miles Davis at the 'Salle Pleyel.' 1949; Page 190: Jean Seberg and Romain Gary; Page 197: LP, Jane Birkin/Serge Gainsbourg; Page 202 and 203: Pauline Réage and Jean Paulhan; Page 210: The Sexual Life of Catherine M, Collection of John Baxter; Page 217: Alain Bernardin and Lava Moor, Collection of John Baxter; Page 222: Princes Diana and Dodi Memorial at Harrods, 2011, ©Museyon; Page 228: John Baxter and Marie Dominique with daughter Louise at their wedding.

ABOUT MUSEYON

Named after the Mouseion, the ancient library of Alexandria, Museyon is a New York City-based independent publisher that explores cultural obsessions such as art, history and travel. Expertly curated and carefully researched, Museyon books offer rich entertainment, with fascinating anecdotes, beautiful images and quality information.

Also Available by **JOHN BAXTER**

CHRONICLES OF OLD PARIS

Exploring the Historic City of Light

THE GOLDEN MOMENTS OF PARIS

A Guide to the Paris of the 1920s

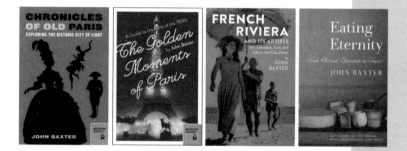

FRENCH RIVIERA AND ITS ARTISTS

Art, Literature, Love, and Life on the Côte d'Azur

EATING ETERNITY

Food, Art and Literature in France

Pick up your copy at wherever books are sold!

www.museyon.com